Jane's

POCKET GUIDE

FIGHTERS OF WORLD WAR II

HarperCollins*Publishers*

In the USA for information address:
HarperCollinsPublishers Inc.
10 East 53rd Street
New York
NY 10022

In the UK for information address:
HarperCollinsPublishers
77-85 Fulham Palace Road
Hammersmith
London W6 8JB

First Published in Great Britain by HarperCollinsPublishers 1999

1 3 5 7 9 10 8 6 4 2

© Tony Holmes 1999

ISBN 0 00 472221 3

Design: Rod Teasdale

Colour reproduction by Colorscan
Printed in Italy

Jane's

POCKET GUIDE

FIGHTERS OF
WORLD WAR II

TONY HOLMES

HarperCollins*Publishers*

Contents

Contents

Contents

Introduction

During World War 2, roughly 160 different types of combat aircraft saw frontline service, or actively participated in the global conflict. Of this number, well over half can be classified as 'fighters'. Seen as the ultimate in winged perfection, the fighter, and its pilot, has consistently grabbed the headlines in the propaganda 'war' fought for the 'hearts and minds' of the various nations embroiled in the major conflicts of the 20th century.

Proof of this is easy to obtain. Just ask anybody to name an aircraft from World War 2, and the trio most usually volunteered are the Spitfire, Messerschmitt (not usually mark-specific, but generally recognised as the Bf 109) and the Mustang. I grant you that these three aircraft are undoubtedly amongst the most important fighter types to see action during 'WW 2', and that between them, their total production amounted to more than 70,000 units in less than a decade of production. However, what of the remaining 80+ aircraft that meet the criterion of 'fighter' during the 1939-45 period? That is where this modest handbook comes in.

Featuring no fewer than 93 entries, this all-new addition to Jane's 'pocket guide' series details all the major fighter types of both the Allied and Axis powers, listing performance data, dimensions, armament and operators, as well as providing a concise history of the aircraft in question. Only those aeroplanes that actually saw action are included in this volume, ranging from the P.Z.L P.11cs and Bf 110B/Cs that engaged each other over Poland in the opening days of World War 2, to the F4U-4s and N1K2-Js that slugged it out over Tokyo Bay in mid-August 1945.

Aside from the text, each fighter type is illustrated with a carefully chosen contemporary black and white photograph that clearly shows its salient details. These images have been specially sourced by the author from the extensive private collections of Philip Jarrett and Bruce Robertson, and have been selected for their clarity and rarity. With each photograph featured over a full page, they clearly show the sheer diversity of the designs that fought for the control of the skies over war-torn Europe, North Africa, the Far East and the Pacific South-West.

I gratefully acknowledge the assistance of both Philip and Bruce, who generously allowed me unrestricted access to their respective collections. This volume would be much the poorer without their photographs – this is a 'guide' book after all! My long-suffering editor, Ian Drury, also deserves huge praise for once again keeping his composure in the face of my liberal interpretation of the publishing term 'deadline'.

Finally, 'thank you' to my wife Katy, who has once again been forced into 'single parent' mode with our own little 13-month-old 'Stuka dive-bomber', Thomas Anthony, whilst 'Daddy' attempted to meet his contractual obligations . . .

Tony Holmes

Bell P-39 Airacobra USA

Type: single-engined monoplane fighter   **Accommodation:** pilot

Development/History

Bell's revolutionary P-39 introduced the concept of both the centrally-mounted powerplant and the tricycle undercarriage to single-engined fighters, the aircraft's unusual configuration stemming from its principal armament, the propeller hub-mounted T9 37 mm cannon. In order to allow the weapon to be housed in the nose the P-39's engine was moved aft to sit virtually over the rear half of the wing centre-section. This drastically shifted the aircraft's centre of gravity, thus forcing designers to adopt a tricycle undercarriage. Unfortunately, the P-39's radical design was not matched by stunning performance figures particularly at heights exceeding 14,000 ft, its normally-aspirated Allison V-1710 struggling in the 'thinner' air at these altitudes – following a service evaluation of the YP-39 in 1938-39, Bell was told by USAAC and NACA officials that a turbocharged version of the V-1710 then available for the Airacobra was not needed! Once the fighter entered service in 1941 the wisdom of this decision was quickly called into question. Indeed, so compromised was the aircraft's 'combatability' in its designated role that it was soon relegated to close air support

duties in theatres where other aircraft could be employed as fighters. Operating at much lower altitudes over the Eastern Front, the Soviet air force did, however, achieve great aerial success with the Bell fighter, utilising some 5000 from 1942 onwards.

Specification

Dimensions:
Length: 30 ft 2 in (9.19 m)
Wingspan: 34 ft 0 in (10.36 m)
Height: 11 ft 10 in (3.61 m)

Weights:
Empty: 5645 lb (2560 kg)
Max T/O: 8300 lb (3765 kg)

Performance:
Max Speed: 386 mph (621 kmh)
Range: 650 miles (1046 km)
Powerplant: Allison V-1710-85
Output: 1200 hp (895 kW)

Armament:
P-39D/N - one 37 mm cannon and two 0.50 in machine guns in nose, two or four 0.30 in machine guns in wings, one 500 lb (227 kg) bomb
P-39Q - two underwing 0.50 in machine guns replaced wing-mounted 0.30 in guns

First Flight Date:
6 April 1938 (XP-39)

Operators:
Australia, France, Italy, Portugal, UK, USA, USSR

Production:
9594

Right: Early-build Bell
P-39D Airacobra

Bell P-63 Kingcobra USA

Type: single-engined monoplane fighter   **Accommodation:** pilot

Development/History

Although the P-63 looked like an enlarged
Airacobra, it was in fact an all-new design that
had a superior turn of speed at all altitudes.
Dubbed the Kingcobra, the fighter drew heavily
on modifications incorporated into the P-39's
original replacement, the cancelled XP-39E.
However, unlike the latter design, the P-63 was
more than just an Airacobra fuselage with new
semi-laminar flow wings – the fighter was
appreciably larger, and boasted an Allison V-
1710-93 engine (P-63A) that could be boosted
to 1500 hp in flight in the event of an
emergency. Although some 3300 were built in
several different versions, by the time the first
production examples began to reach the USAAF
in October 1943, the P-51B, P-38H and P-47C
had successfully filled the air force's
requirement for a frontline fighter. Most P-63s
were therefore made available for lend-lease
purchase, and the Soviet air force happily
snapped up 2400 examples. A further 300 went
to Free French units in the Mediterranean, but
the primary customer – the USAAF – restricted
their use of the Kingcobra to training
squadrons in America. The final variant in
production at war's end was the P-63E, of

Specification

Dimensions:
Length: 32 ft 8 in (9.96 m)
Wingspan: 38 ft 4 in (11.68 m)
Height: 12 ft 7 in (3.84 m)

Weights:
Empty: 6375 lb (2892 kg)
Max T/O: 10 500 lb (4763 kg)

Performance:
Max Speed: 410 mph (660 kmh)
Range: 2200 miles (3540 km) with external fuel
tanks
Powerplant: Allison V-1710-93
Output: 1325 hp (988 kW)

Armament:
one 37 mm cannon and two 0.50 in machine
guns in nose, two underwing 0.50 in machine
guns, up to three 500 lb (227 kg) bombs

First Flight Date:
7 December 1942

Operators:
France, USA, USSR

Production:
3303

which only 13 out of an order for 2930
had been delivered when the contract
was cancelled in the wake of VJ-Day.

*Right: Bell P-63C
Kingcobra serial
number 311720*

Bell P-59 Airacomet USA

Type: twin-engined monoplane jet fighter

Accommodation: pilot

Development/History

America's first jet fighter, the Bell P-59 was built around the revolutionary Whittle turbojet, unveiled to the US Government by Britain in September 1941. Of conventional design, with a straight wing, the Bell fighter was powered by two Americanised General Electric Type IAs (subsequently redesignated J31). Flight development went smoothly, with three prototypes (XP-59A) and 13 evaluation airframes (YP-59A) being delivered by late 1944. It was soon realised at an early stage of the flight development programme that the Airacomet boasted a performance inferior to many frontline piston-engined fighters of the day, so production aircraft subsequently acquired were relegated to the fighter trainer role. First production P-59A was delivered to the USAAF in August 1944 and 20 were built, of which three went to the US Navy as the XF2L-1. The P-59B replaced the A-model soon after, and a further 30 were delivered before the remaining 50 on order (plus an expected follow-on batch of a further 250) were cancelled in October 1944.

Specification

Dimensions:
Length: 38 ft 10 in (11.83 m)
Wingspan: 45 ft 6 in (13.97 m)
Height: 12 ft 4 in (3.76 m)

Weights:
Empty: 8165 lb (3704 kg)
Max T/O: 13 700 lb (6214 kg)

Performance:
Max Speed: 413 mph (665 kmh)
Range: 525 miles (845 km)
Powerplants: two General Electric J31-GE-3/5 turbojets
Output: 4000 lb st (18.0 kN)

Armament:
one 37 mm cannon and three 0.50 in machine guns in nose, two underwing racks for bombs or drop tanks

First Flight Date:
1 October 1942

Operators:
UK and USA

Production:
66

Right: First production P-59A-1 44-22609 first formates with P-63A 42-69417

Bloch MB.152 France

Type: single-engined monoplane fighter   Accommodation: pilot

Development/History

The most populous member of the Bloch MB.150 family of single-seat fighters developed in the second half of the 1930s, the MB.152 combined the proven all-metal structure of the MB.151 with the latest version of Gnome-Rhône's tried and tested 14N radial engine. Better armament was also fitted to the new Bloch fighter, and the first of 482 built for the *Armée de l'Air* entered service in April 1939. Subsequent deliveries proved to be slow, however, and those in the frontline suffered from poor serviceability. Nevertheless, no fewer than nine fighter groups possessed MB.152s at the time of the German invasion of France on 10 May 1940, and although the fighter suffered heavy attrition (86 were lost in action), MB.152 pilots were credited with the destruction of 146 enemy aircraft prior to France's capitulation on 30 June 1940. The aircraft continued to see service with the Vichy French for a further two years, whilst small numbers also flew with the Luftwaffe and the Romanian air force.

Specification

Dimensions:
Length: 29 ft 10 in (9.10 m)
Wingspan: 34 ft 7 in (10.54 m)
Height: 9 ft 11 in (3.02 m)

Weights:
Empty: 4758 lb (2158 kg)
Max T/O: 6173 lb (2800 kg)

Performance:
Max Speed: 320 mph (515 kmh)
Range: 525 miles (845 km)
Powerplant: Gnome-Rhône GR 14N-25
Output: 1080 hp (806 kW)

Armament:
two 20 mm cannon and two 7.5 mm machine guns in nose, or four 7.5 mm machine guns in wings

First Flight Date:
15 December 1938

Operators:
France, Germany, Greece, Romania

Production:
482

Right: This Bloch 152 of the Armée de l'Air was photographed in the early months of World War 2

Boulton Paul Defiant UK

Type: single-engined monoplane fighter

Accommodation: pilot and turret gunner

Development/History

The final result of the turret fighter concept evolved by the RAF in the early 1930s, the Defiant enjoyed a less than successful career as a frontline fighter in the dangerous skies over southern England during the summer of 1940. Built to combine the strengths of new monoplane fighter design with the latest in turret weaponry, the Defiant struggled against single-seat opposition both in terms of speed and agility due to the weight of its two-man crew and its primary armament. Entering squadron service in December 1939, the aircraft initially enjoyed some success against German opposition surprised by its turret armament. However, once these same pilots learned that the aircraft had no forward-firing guns, they tailored their tactics accordingly and inflicted heavy losses on the Defiant units. Removed from daylight operations in August 1940, surviving Defiant Is and new Mk IIs in turn equipped 13 newly-formed nightfighter squadrons, and between the autumn of 1940 and early 1942, the aircraft enjoyed some nocturnal success.

Specification

Dimensions:
Length: 35 ft 4 in (10.77 m)
Wingspan: 39 ft 4 in (12.00 m)
Height: 12 ft 2 in (3.70 m)

Weights:
Empty: 6078 lb (2757 kg)
Max T/O: 8318 lb (3773 kg)

Performance:
Max Speed: 304 mph (489 kmh)
Range: 465 miles (748 km)
Powerplant: Rolls-Royce Merlin III
Output: 1030 hp (768 kW)

Armament:
four 0.303 in machine guns in dorsal turret

First Flight Date:
11 August 1937

Operator:
UK

Production:
1075

Right: Boulton Paul Defiant II AA436 of No 151 Sqn

Brewster Buffalo USA

Type: single-engined monoplane fighter

Accommodation: pilot

Development/History

The first monoplane fighter to enter service with the US Navy, the Buffalo was designed for use aboard aircraft carriers. The first aircraft delivered to the navy were Wright Cyclone-powered 11 F2A-1s, which were taken on strength in June 1939. Part of an order for 54 such aircraft, the remaining 43 Buffalos were instead supplied to the Finnish air force as the Model B-239. The follow-on F2A-2 and -3 proved more popular with the US Navy, as they featured the definitive Wright 1820-40 radial engine and armour protection. These latter variants were also ordered as B-339B/D/Es by the Belgian, The Netherlands East Indies and British governments. Although enjoying little success with any of these Allied air forces in combat against the Japanese in 1941-42, the Buffalo exacted a heavy toll on the Soviet Red Air Force in the hands of Finnish fighter pilots between 1941-44.

Specification

Dimensions:
Length: 26 ft 4 in (8.03 m)
Wingspan: 35 ft 0 in (10.67 m)
Height: 12 ft 1 in (3.68 m)

Weights:
Empty: 4732 lb (2146 kg)
Max T/O: 7159 lb (3247 kg)

Performance:
Max Speed: 321 mph (516 kmh)
Range: 965 miles (1553 km)
Powerplant: Wright R-1820-40
Output: 1200 hp (895 kW)

Armament:
four 0.303 in machine guns, two in the nose and one in each wing

First Flight Date:
December 1937

Operators:
Australia, Finland, The Netherlands East Indies, New Zealand, UK, USA

Production:
509

Right: RAF Brewster Buffalo I AS426 seen in February 1941

Bristol Beaufighter UK

Type: twin-engined monoplane fighter   **Accommodation:** pilot and navigator/gunner

Development/History

Built as a private venture by Bristol using the wings tail and rear fuselage of the company's rugged Beaufort torpedo bomber, the Beaufighter proved to be one of the best strike and night fighters of World War 2. Boasting a new main fuselage, powerful Hercules (and later Merlin) engines and a mixed gun and cannon armament, the first Beaufighter entered RAF service in September 1940. Soon fitted with radar, the Mk IF (and Merlin-powered Mk IIF) took the fight to the Luftwaffe during its nocturnal blitz of 1940-41. Further developed into the Mk VIF in 1942, this version of the Beaufighter had air intercept (AI) radar fitted in a 'thimble' nose cone. Issued to 14 fighter squadrons and four USAAF units in the Mediterranean, the Mk VIF remained an important asset until mid-1944. The long-range dayfighter variants also proved a staple aircraft for Coastal Command, the Mk IC, VIC and TF X seeing service off the coasts of Occupied Europe from Norway to southern France, throughout the Mediterranean and North Africa, and against the Japanese in the Far East.

Specification (all dimensions and performance data for Mk IF)

Dimensions:
Length: 41 ft 4 in (12.60 m)
Wingspan: 57 ft 10 in (17.63 m)
Height: 15 ft 10 in (4.83 m)

Weights:
Empty: 14 069 lb (6382 kg)
Max T/O: 21 100 lb (9571 kg)

Performance:
Max Speed: 323 mph (520 kmh)
Range: 1170 miles (1883 km)
Powerplants: two Bristol Hercules III or XI engines
Output: 2980 hp (2088 kW) or 3180 hp (2370 kW) respectively

Armament:
four 20 mm cannon in nose and six 0.303 in machine guns in wing

First Flight Date:
17 July 1939

Operators:
Australia, Canada, New Zealand, South Africa, UK, USA

Production:
5949 (all versions)

Right: Bristol Beaufighter Mk IF T4638 of No 604 Sqn

CAC Boomerang Australia

Type: single-engined monoplane fighter   **Accommodation:** pilot

Development/History

The only Australian-designed fighter aircraft to ever see combat, the Boomerang was designed and built in record time in the wake of the Japanese raid on Pearl Harbor. Realising that neither the British or American governments could spare valuable fighter aircraft to stem the Japanese tide in south-east Asia, the Australians set about producing their own home-built machine. The result was the Commonwealth Aircraft Corporation (CAC) CA-12 Boomerang, which took to the skies for the first time just 16 weeks and three days after its design had been approved. Constructed around the largest engine then built in Australia (the Twin Wasp), and incorporating as many components from the semi-indigenous Wirraway trainer/dive-bomber as possible, the Boomerang boasted marvellous manoeuvrability but poor straight-line speed. It was therefore relegated to the army support role when it reached the frontline in mid-1943, the USAAF having since arrived in-theatre with vastly superior fighters. Some 250 Boomerangs were eventually built by the CAC, and the aircraft performed valuable work over the mountainous terrain of New Guinea, usually operating under army control.

Specification

Dimensions:
Length: 25 ft 6 in (7.77 m)
Wingspan: 36 ft 0 in (10.97 m)
Height: 9 ft 7 in (2.92 m)

Weights:
Empty: 5373 lb (2437 kg)
Max T/O: 7699 lb (3492 kg)

Performance:
Max Speed: 302 mph (486 kmh)
Range: 930 miles (1497 km)
Powerplant: Pratt & Whitney R-1830-S3C4-G Twin Wasp
Output: 1200 hp (894 kW)

Armament:
two 20 mm cannon and four 0.303 in machine guns in wing; four 20 lb (9 kg) smoke bombs under wings

First Flight Date:
28 May 1942

Operator:
Australia

Production:
250

Right: CAC CA-13
Boomerang A46-126
of No 5 Sqn

Curtiss P-36/Hawk 75 USA

Type: single-engined monoplane fighter   **Accommodation:** pilot

Development/History

Forerunner of the famous 'Hawk' series of fighters produced in great numbers by Curtiss during World War 2, the original Model 75 was the losing design in a competition fly-off held by the USAAC for a new monoplane fighter in mid-1935. Beaten by the Seversky P-35, the Curtiss design was overhauled by the company primarily through the fitment of a more powerful Twin Wasp engine. The resulting Y1P-36 was ordered into production in 1936, and by the time of the Pearl Harbor raid on 7 December 1941, some 209 P-36A/Cs had been delivered to the USAAC. Export orders were also received by Curtiss for their fighter, designated the Hawk 75, and large numbers were bought by a clutch of nations, including around 350 (out of an order for 620) for the French – the latter were credited with destroying some 311 German aircraft during the Battle of France. The remaining aircraft not delivered to the French were issued instead to the RAF, and they subsequently saw action in the Far East against the Japanese in 1942-43.

Specification

Dimensions:
Length: 28 ft 6 in (8.69 m)
Wingspan: 37 ft 3.5 in (11.37 m)
Height: 12 ft 2 in (3.71 m)

Weights:
Empty: 4567 lb (2072 kg)
Max T/O: 6010 lb (2726 kg)

Performance:
Max Speed: 300 mph (483 kmh)
Range: 825 miles (1328 km)
Powerplant: Pratt & Whitney R-1830-13 Twin Wasp
Output: 1050 hp (783 kW)

Armament:
one 0.30 in and one 0.50 in machine guns in nose, with additional two 0.30 in machine guns in wings; Hawk 75A had up to six machine guns, and provision for 400 lb (181 kg) of underwing bombs

First Flight Date:
15 May 1935 (Model 75) and February 1937 (Y1P-36)

Operators:
Argentina, China, Finland, France, The Netherlands East Indies, Norway, Peru, Portugal, South Africa, Thailand, UK, USA

Production:
1424

Right: Curtiss Hawk 75A-7 of The Netherlands East Indies Air Force's 1.Vliegtuigafdeling

Curtiss P-40 Tomahawk USA

Type: single-engined monoplane fighter   **Accommodation:** pilot

Development/History

Developed simply by replacing the P-36's Twin Wasp radial with a supercharged Allison V-1710 inline engine, the XP-40 prototype impressed the USAAC so much that an order for 524 aircraft was placed in early 1939. This was the largest contract for aircraft issued to a contractor since the Great War, and the first production aircraft flew in April 1940. A large number of P-40B/Cs (no A-models were ever built) had been delivered to the USAAC by 7 December 1941, and these initially took the fight to the Japanese, but were soon shown to be inferior to enemy fighters. Aside from USAAC use, the Curtiss design also saw much action with the RAF, which christened it the Tomahawk. No fewer than 1180 fighters were acquired by the British, and these were in turn used by RAF, RCAF, RAAF and South African units primarily in North Africa and the Middle East in 1941-42. Around 100 of these ex-British aircraft were also issued to the American Volunteer Group (dubbed the 'Flying Tigers') in China and Burma at around the same time.

Specification

Dimensions:
Length: 31 ft 8.5 in (9.66 m)
Wingspan: 37 ft 3.5 in (11.37 m)
Height: 10 ft 7 in (3.22 m)

Weights:
Empty: 5812 lb (2636 kg)
Max T/O: 8058 lb (3655 kg)

Performance:
Max Speed: 345 mph (555 kmh)
Range: 1230 miles (1979 km) with external drop tank
Powerplant: Allison V-1710-33
Output: 1040 hp (775 kW)

Armament:
two 0.50 in machine guns in nose and two or four 0.30 in machine guns in wings

First Flight Date:
14 October 1938

Operators:
Australia, Canada, China, Egypt, South Africa, Turkey, UK, USA, USSR

Production:
1703

Right: RAF Curtiss Tomahawk IIB AH925

Curtiss P-40 Kittyhawk/Warhawk USA

Type: single-engined monoplane fighter   **Accommodation:** pilot

Development/History

With the further development of the Allison V-1710, Curtiss kept pace on the airframe side by producing the P-40D/E in 1941. The primary differences between these models and the earlier B/C centred on a drastically revised nose shape due to the chin radiator being moved forward, which in turn allowed the propeller thrust line to be raised, the undercarriage to be shortened and fuselage top line to be lowered and recontoured. The modifications to the forward fuselage also meant that the nose guns were moved to the wings, changing from 0.30 in to 0.50 in in the process. As with the Tomahawk, the RAF was a major export customer for the aircraft, which it christened the Kittyhawk. Other users also included the RCAF, RAAF and the South African air force. In USAAF service, the aircraft received the appellation Warhawk, and subsequent variants of the fighter were powered by Packard Merlins as well as Allison V-1710s. The last P-40 (an N-model) was built by Curtiss in December 1944.

Specification

(all dimensions and performance data for P-40E)

Dimensions:

Length: 33 ft 4 in (10.16 m)

Wingspan: 37 ft 4 in (11.38 m)

Height: 12 ft 4 in (3.76 m)

Weights:

Empty: 6300 lb (2858 kg)

Max T/O: 9100 lb (4128 kg)

Performance:

Max Speed: 335 mph (539 kmh)

Range: 900 miles (1448 km) with external drop tank

Powerplant: Allison V-1710-39

Output: 1150 hp (857 kW)

Armament:

six 0.50 in machine guns in wings; one 500 lb (227 kg) bomb under fuselage or two 100 lb (45 kg) under wings

First Flight Date:

22 May 1941

Operators:

Australia, Canada, China, France, The Netherlands East Indies, New Zealand, South Africa, UK, USA, USSR

Production:

12 029

Right: RAF Kittyhawk IV (P-40N)

de Havilland Mosquito UK

Type: twin-engined monoplane fighter

Accommodation: pilot and navigator

Development/History

Built to replace the ageing Blenheim, the Mosquito flew very much in the face of convention by utilising a wooden fuselage and wings. Initially rejected by the Air Ministry in the autumn of 1938 on the grounds of its unorthodox construction, the aircraft's wooden structure actually ensured its series production with the outbreak of war due to the fear that the supply of light alloys from abroad would be affected by the conflict. The prototype Mosquito fighter took to the skies 14 months later, the sleek Merlin-powered design soon proving its worth during flight trials. The first Mosquito fighter variant to see operational service was the F/NF II, which began to reach the frontline in January 1942. Over the next two years the Mosquito gradually replaced the Beaufighter as the RAF's premier nightfighter, with the radar-equipped NF XIII and NF 30 being the ultimate wartime variants. In the day fighter-bomber role, the FB VI proved so successful that it became the most important Mosquito version, at least in terms of number built (2257 in the UK), of them all.

Specification (all dimensions and performance data for F II)

Dimensions:
Length: 40 ft 10 in (12.44 m)
Wingspan: 54 ft 2 in (16.51 m)
Height: 15 ft 3 in (4.65 m)

Weights:
Empty: 14 300 lb (6486 kg)
Max T/O: 20 000 lb (9072 kg)

Performance:
Max Speed: 370 mph (595 kmh)
Range: 1770 miles (2848 km) with external drop tanks
Powerplants: two Rolls-Royce Merlin 23 engines
Output: 2920 hp (2176 kW)

Armament:
four 20 mm cannon and four 0.303 in machine guns in nose

First Flight Date:
15 May 1941 (F II)

Operators:
Australia, Canada, New Zealand, UK, USA

Production:
4627 (fighter and fighter-bomber variants only)

Right: Mosquito NF II DD737

Dewoitine D.250 France

Type: single-engined monoplane fighter   Accommodation: pilot

Development/History

Undoubtedly the best French fighter in service at the time of the German invasion in May 1940, the D.520 had been designed to meet an *Armée de l'Air* requirement for a monoplane fighter issued in 1936. Unfortunately for France, the first examples of the Dewoitine fighter only began to reach the frontline in December 1939, these aircraft being part of an order for 2300 D.520s. Production rates were poor, and by the eve of the *Blitzkrieg*, just 36 fighters had made it into squadron service. However, the invasion spurred a massive production programme, and by the Armistice on 30 June, 437 had been built. No further D.520s were built until June 1941, when the Vichy government ordered Dewoitine to re-open the production line. A further 478 were then produced until construction ceased in mid-1943. Aside from its use by the French both before and after capitulation, the D.520 was also employed as a fighter trainer by the Luftwaffe, and others were issued to Italy, Bulgaria and Romania in the wake of the French surrender in 1940. As a fighter, the D.520 enjoyed some success, being credited with 114 German aircraft destroyed during the Battle of France, plus further kills (against Allied aircraft) in Vichy hands in North Africa and Syria in 1941-42.

Specification

Dimensions:
Length: 28 ft 8.5 in (8.76 m)
Wingspan: 33 ft 5.5 in (10.20 m)
Height: 8 ft 5 in (2.56 m)

Weights:
Empty: 4612 lb (2092 kg)
Max T/O: 6129 lb (2780 kg)

Performance:
Max Speed: 329 mph (529 kmh)
Range: 777 miles (1250 km)
Powerplant: Hispano-Suiza 12Y-45
Output: 910 hp (678 kW)

Armament:
one 20 mm cannon firing through propeller hub and four 7.5 mm machine guns in wing

First Flight Date:
2 October 1938

Operators:
Bulgaria, France, Germany, Italy, Romania

Production:
918

Right: Newly-built Dewoitine D.520 of the Vichy French Armée de l'Air in 1941

Dornier Do 217J/N Germany

Type: twin-engined monoplane fighter   Accommodation: three-/four-man crew

Development/History

The ultimate Dornier nightfighters, the Do 217J/N owed much to the company's previous experience with the Do 17Z *Kauz* and Do 215B-5 *Kauz 3*. Both earlier types had enjoyed varied levels of success with the Luftwaffe's continually expanding *Nachtjagd*, and with the arrival of the latter variants in 1942, the German nightfighter force could truly boast a heavyweight nocturnal intruder. The FuG 202 *Lichtenstein* BC radar-equipped J-2 was the primary operational variant of 1942-43, partially equipping eight *gruppen* until phased out in 1944. Twelve J-models were also supplied to the Italians in 1943 to help defend the northern industrial centres of Turin, Genoa and Milan. The final variant to enter service was the N-1/-2, this model having the turret, ventral gun and bomb bay removed, but utilising an upgraded version of the FuG 202 radar. Like the J-model, it too was removed from the frontline in early 1944, the stopgap Dornier nightfighters having been replaced by more nimble Ju 88s and Bf 110s as production of the latter types began to keep pace with demand. A total of 15 gruppen operated the Do 217J/N during its brief service life, flying these converted bombers in Defence of the Reich, Eastern Front and Mediterranean operations alongside Bf 110s and Ju 88s.

Specification (all dimensions and performance data for Do 217J)

Dimensions:
Length: 59 ft 0 in (18.00 m)
Wingspan: 62 ft 4 in (19.00 m)
Height: 16 ft 3 in (4.97 m)

Weights:
Empty: 20 613 lb (9350 kg)
Max T/O: 29 056 lb (13 180 kg)

Performance:
Max Speed: 304 mph (489 kmh)
Range: 1305 miles (2100 km)
Powerplants: two BMW 801A engines
Output: 3160 hp (2356 kW)

Armament:
four 7.9 mm machine guns or 20 mm cannon in nose, 13 mm machine gun in dorsal turret, aft firing 13 mm machine gun in ventral gondola, and bomb bay retained in certain variants

First Flight Date:
late 1941

Operators:
Germany and Italy

Production:
364

Right: This Dornier Do 217J-2 served as a manufacturer's trials aircraft

Douglas P-70/DB-7 Havoc USA

Type: twin-engined monoplane fighter

Accommodation: pilot and navigator

Development/History

First developed as a makeshift nightfighter by the RAF in Havoc I form in 1940, the Douglas 'medium twin' proved relatively effective in the early war years in this specialist role. Chosen by the British because it was one of the few aircraft that could accommodate the cumbersome early AI radar and still boast an adequate performance as a fighter, the Havoc Is were converted from around 100 ex-French contract DB-7s that had not been delivered prior to France's surrender in June 1940. A number of Havocs were also equipped with the Turbinlite searchlight in the extreme nose, these unarmed aircraft operating in unison with Hurricane or Defiant nightfighters. Only moderately successful, the Havoc I/IIs had been replaced by Beaufighters by 1942. The USAAF's P-70 followed the RAF's Havoc I lead, and was built in modest numbers as an interim nightfighter, pending the arrival of the awesome P-61 Black Widow in 1944. Used operationally by four squadrons in the Pacific, limited success was enjoyed by the AI Mk IV radar-equipped P-70s. Further A-20G/Js were equipped with SCR-720/-729 radar and used as nightfighter trainers in the USA in 1943-44.

Specification (all dimensions and performance data for P-70)

Dimensions:
Length: 47 ft 7 in (14.50 m)
Wingspan: 61 ft 4 in (18.69 m)
Height: 17 ft 7 in (5.36 m)

Weights:
Empty: 16 031 lb (7272 kg)
Max T/O: 21 264 lb (9645 kg)

Performance:
Max Speed: 329 mph (529 kmh)
Range: 1060 miles (1696 km)
Powerplants: two Wright R-2600-11 Double Cyclone engines
Output: 3200 hp (2386 kW)

Armament:
six 0.50 in machine guns in ventral tray or similar number in nose

First Flight Date:
early 1941

Operators:
UK and USA

Production:
approximately 500

Right: Douglas P-70
serial number 39-776

Fairey Fulmar UK

Type: single-engined monoplane fighter

Accommodation: pilot and observer/gunner

Development/History

Directly developed from the P.4/34 light bomber of 1937 through the addition of folding wings, a catapult spool and an arrestor hook, amongst other additions, the Fulmar gave the Royal Navy its first eight-gun fighter when it entered service in May 1940. Thrust into action within months protecting Malta convoys from the deck of HMS *Illustrious*, the fighter provided sterling service with 11 Fleet Air Arm squadrons, particularly against Italian and German opponents in the Mediterranean in 1941-42. Aside from its use in this theatre, the Fulmar also saw action off Norway and Ceylon, and completed its frontline service as a nightfighter protecting Russian convoys in 1944-45. The last Fulmar (a tropicalised Mk II, fitted with a Merlin 30 engine) was delivered in February 1943, and by this stage of the war, most Fleet Air Arm fighter units had replaced the Fairey fighter with Seafires or Corsair Is. Aside from its frontline role, the Fulmar also proved ideally suited to deck landing training, as its vice-free handling qualities and slow stalling speed made it easy to operate 'around the boat'.

Specification (all dimensions and performance data for Fulmar Mk I)

Dimensions:
Length: 40 ft 3 in (12.27 m)
Wingspan: 46 ft 4.5 in (14.13 m)
Height: 10 ft 8 in (3.25 m)

Weights:
Empty: 6915 lb (3137 kg)
Max T/O: 9800 lb (4445 kg)

Performance:
Max Speed: 256 mph (412 kmh)
Range: 830 miles (1335 km)
Powerplant: Rolls-Royce Merlin VIII
Output: 1080 hp (805 kW)

Armament:
eight 0.303 in machine guns in wings; optional single 0.303 in machine gun in rear cockpit; two 250 lb (113 kg) bombs under wings

First Flight Date:
4 January 1940

Operator:
UK

Production:
600

Right: Fairey Fulmar Mk I N1858

Fairey Firefly UK

Type: single-engined monoplane fighter   **Accommodation:** pilot and observer/gunner

Development/History

The Royal Navy got such good all-round service from the Fulmar that it contracted Fairey to work on a successor as early as 1940. Using the familiar Fleet Air Arm sobriquet of Firefly, the new fighter began to reach the fleet in March of 1943 in F I fighter-bomber form. Powered by a Griffon engine, the Firefly first saw action in July 1944 when squadrons from HMS *Indefatigable* participated in a series of raids aimed at sinking the German battleship *Tirpitz*, moored in a Norwegian fjord. Later that same year the aircraft commenced a sustained period of combat against Japanese targets in the Indian and Pacific Oceans. The oil refineries on Sumatra were particularly hard hit by Fleet Air Arm squadrons in early 1945, and Firefly units were in the forefront of these missions. Aside from the fighter-bomber variant, radar-equipped FR I photo-recce and NF I/II nightfighter Fireflies also saw action in the final months of the war. Postwar, the heavily revised Firefly Mk IV was built in great numbers (as were several other subsequent variants) from 1946 through to 1950, and it saw action in Korea with both the British and Australian navies, as well as service with a handful of other operators.

Specification (all dimensions and performance data for Firefly Mk I)

Dimensions:
Length: 37 ft 7.25 in (11.46 m)
Wingspan: 44 ft 6 in (13.56 m)
Height: 13 ft 7 in (4.14 m)

Weights:
Empty: 9750 lb (4423 kg)
Max T/O: 14 020 lb (6359 kg)

Performance:
Max Speed: 319 mph (513 kmh)
Range: 1070 miles (1722 km)
Powerplant: Rolls-Royce Griffon IIB
Output: 1730 hp (1290 kW)

Armament:
four 20 mm cannon in wings; provision for two 1000 lb (454 kg) bombs or eight 60 lb (27 kg) rockets under wings

First Flight Date:
22 December 1941

Operator:
UK

Production:
842 (wartime only)

Right: Fairey Firefly F I
Z2035

Fiat CR.32 Italy

Type: single-engined biplane fighter   **Accommodation:** pilot

Development/History

Developed from the CR.30 frontline fighter built in small numbers for the Italian *Regia Aeronautica* in 1933-34, the CR.32 was thoroughly obsolescent by the outbreak of World War 2, yet was still in more widespread use in 1940 than any other Italian fighter type. Like all Fiat biplane fighters, the CR.32 was highly manoeuvrable, and it also enjoyed some success in export markets in the final years of peace. Extensively used by General Franco's Nationalist forces during the Spanish Civil War, the CR.32 also saw action in China during the second Sino-Japanese war, in Hungary as part of the Carpathian dispute and finally in Paraguay during the Gran Chaco war. The final examples left Fiat in 1939, although 100 licence-built CR.32 (designated HA-132-L Chirris) were built by Hispano-Suiza between 1940-43. Some 400 CR.32 remained in service with the *Regia Aeronautica* in late 1939, and the fighter saw much action in the Greek and East African campaigns in the close support and nightfighter roles. Surviving fighters were finally relegated to training and secondary roles in late 1941.

Specification

Dimensions:

Length: 24 ft 5.5 in (7.45 m)

Wingspan: 31 ft 2 in (9.50 m)

Height: 8 ft 11 in (2.72 m)

Weights:

Empty: 3042 lb (1380 kg)

Max T/O: 4200 lb (1905 kg)

Performance:

Max Speed: 221 mph (357 kmh)

Range: 485 miles (780 km)

Powerplant: Fiat A 30 RA

Output: 600 hp (447 kW)

Armament:

two 12.7 mm machine guns in nose; CR.32bis two 12.7 mm machine guns in nose and two 7.7 mm machine guns in wings; one 220 lb (100 kg) or two 110 lb (50 kg) bombs under wings

First Flight Date:

28 April 1933

Operators:

Austria, China, Hungary, Italy, Paraguay, Spain, Venezuela

Production:

1272

Right: Fiat CR.32quater of the Regia Aeronautica

Fiat CR.42 Falco Italy

Type: single-engined biplane fighter   Accommodation: pilot

Development/History

The last Fiat biplane fighter (and effectively the last of its type in the world), the Falco, like the CR.32, was obsolete before the outbreak of World War 2. Despite this, great numbers saw action during the conflict not only with the Italians, but also the Finns, Germans, Hungarians and Belgians. A development of the unsuccessful CR.41, the first CR.42 entered frontline service with the *Regia Aeronautica* in April 1939, followed by a handful of other export countries. Built in four main variants that covered day fighter, nightfighter and close support roles, the CR.42 saw action in the Belgian, Greek, East African, Western European, Mediterranean and North African theatres. As the Fiat fighter became more and more vulnerable in its designed role, survivors were relegated to performing nocturnal patrols over northern Italy. Although production ended in early 1942, small numbers of CR.42 remained in service with the Luftwaffe as night ground attack platforms in the Balkans and northern Italy following the Italian surrender in September 1943.

Specification

Dimensions:
Length: 27 ft 3 in (8.30 m)
Wingspan: 31 ft 10 in (9.70 m)
Height: 10 ft 10 in (3.30 m)

Weights:
Empty: 3763 lb (1707 kg)
Max T/O: 5302 lb (2405 kg)

Performance:
Max Speed: 266 mph (428 kmh)
Range: 630 miles (1014 km) with external fuel tanks
Powerplant: Fiat A 74 RC38
Output: 840 hp (626 kW)

Armament:
two 12.7 mm machine guns in nose; CR.42ter two 12.7 mm machine guns in nose and two 7.7 mm machine guns in wings; CR.42AS two or four 12.7 mm machine guns and two 220 lb (100 kg) bombs under wings

First Flight Date:
23 May 1938

Operators:
Belgium, Finland, Germany, Hungary, Italy, Sweden

Production:
1781

Right: Fiat CR.42 Falco of the Regia Aeronautica

Fiat G.50 Freccia Italy

Type: single-engined monoplane fighter   Accommodation: pilot

Development/History

Built in answer to a 1936 Italian Air Ministry specification, Fiat's G.50 was the very first metal monoplane fighter to enter service with the *Regia Aeronautica*. Utilising the same radial powerplant as fitted to the CR.42, the Freccia made its combat debut in late 1938 when 12 were sent to Spain for evaluation. Pilots quickly criticised is modest armament and enclosed cockpit canopy, and although the next batch of G.50s had no additional guns, they did boast open cockpits. Following the construction of 245 G.50s, production switched to the improved G.50bis in late 1940, the new variant featuring more fuel in self-sealing tanks, increased protective armour, a redesigned fin and rudder and flattened upper fuselage to improve pilot visibility – but still no extra guns. The final series production Freccia was the G.50B, which featured tandem seating for two pilots, and served as an unarmed advanced trainer. Obsolescent by the end of 1940, the G.50 nevertheless saw much action with the *Regia Aeronautica* in western Europe, Greece, the Western Desert, Tunisia and Sicily, before being relegated to local defence duties. Some 35 G.50s also saw considerable action with the

Specification (all dimensions and performance data for G.50bis)

Dimensions:
Length: 27 ft 2 in (8.28 m)
Wingspan: 36 ft 1 in (11.00 m)
Height: 9 ft 9 in (2.97 m)

Weights:
Empty: 4443 lb (2015 kg)
Max T/O: 5560 lb (2522 kg)

Performance:
Max Speed: 293 mph (472 kmh)
Range: 620 miles (998 km)
Powerplant: Fiat A 74 RC38
Output: 840 hp (626 kW)

Armament:
two 12.7 mm machine guns in nose

First Flight Date:
26 February 1937

Operators:
Croatia, Finland, Italy, Spain

Production:
777

Finnish air force during the Continuation War with the USSR between 1941-44, and the survivors remained in service until 1947.

Right: Fiat G.50bis Freccia found abandoned in North Africa in 1942

Fiat G.55 Centauro Italy

Type: single-engined monoplane fighter

Accommodation: pilot

Development/History

Considered by many to be the premier Italian fighter of the war, the G.55 arrived too late to make a major impact on the Allied air forces battering Italy by mid-1943. Designed as a drastically improved G.50, the G.55 utilised a more efficient wing, more slender fuselage, greatly improved armament and, most importantly of all, a licence-built Daimler-Benz DB 605A inline engine. Manufacture of the sole wartime production model (G.55/I) commenced in early 1943, but it was only weeks prior to the Italian surrender that the first Centauros arrived in the frontline. Although the fighter saw no action with the *Regia Aeronautica*, it did, however, fight on with the pro-German *Aeronautica Nazionale Repubblicana*, as the Fiat factory producing the G.55/I was in northern Italy. It partially equipped six fighter *gruppo*, and operated alongside Luftwaffe fighter *gruppen* sent to Italy to help defend the areas remaining in Axis control. Several one-off prototypes were subsequently produced during 1944, but none reached production. In 1947-48 around 60 Centauros were built utilising unfinished wartime

airframes, these aircraft in turn being sold as single-seat fighters and two-seat advanced trainers to Italy, Argentina and Egypt.

Specification

Dimensions:
Length: 30 ft 9 in (9.37 m)
Wingspan: 38 ft 10.5 in (11.85 m)
Height: 10 ft 3.25 in (3.13 m)

Weights:
Empty: 5952 lb (2700 kg)
Max T/O: 8179 lb (3710 kg)

Performance:
Max Speed: 385 mph (620 kmh)
Range: 1025 miles (1650 km) with external fuel tanks
Powerplant: Fiat RA 1050 Tifone (licence-built Daimler-Benz DB 605A)
Output: 1475 hp (1100 kW)

Armament:
one 20 mm cannon in propeller hub, two 12.7 mm machine guns in nose, two 20 mm cannon in wings

First Flight Date:
30 April 1942

Operator:
Italy

Production:
approximately 212

Right: Fiat G.55/I Centauro of 5a Squadriglia, RSI

Focke-Wulf Fw 190A/F/G Germany

Type: single-engined monoplane fighter   Accommodation: pilot

Development/History

Arguably Germany's best fighter of the war, the Fw 190 caught the RAF by surprise when it appeared over the Channel front in 1941. Indeed, the Focke-Wulf fighter remained unmatched in aerial combat until the advent of the Spitfire Mk IX in late 1942. Powered by the superbly compact BMW 801 radial engine, the Fw 190 also boasted excellent handling characteristics to match its turn of speed. The A-model Fw 190s were the dedicated fighter variants of the 'butcher bird', and as the design matured, so more guns were fitted and more power squeezed out of the BMW engine. By the end of 1942, production of the Fw 190 accounted for half of all German fighters built that year, and the fighter-bomber F/G had also been developed – the first F-models entered frontline service on the Eastern Front during the winter of 1942-43. All manner of ordnance from bombs to rockets could be carried by the fighter-bomber Fw 190, and additional protective armour for the pilot was also added around the cockpit. Variants of the Fw 190 saw action against the Allies on all fronts of the war in Europe, and the aircraft remained a deadly opponent for Allied fighter pilots right up to VE-Day.

Specification (all dimensions and performance data for Fw 190A-3)

Dimensions:
Length: 29 ft 0 in (8.84 m)
Wingspan: 34 ft 5.5 in (10.50 m)
Height: 13 ft 0 in (3.96 m)

Weights:
Empty: 6393 lb (2900 kg)
Max T/O: 8770 lb (3978 kg)

Performance:
Max Speed: 382 mph (615 kmh)
Range: 497 miles (800 km)
Powerplant: BMW 801D
Output: 1700 hp (1268 kW)

Armament:
two 7.9 mm machine guns in nose, four 20 mm cannon in wings; provision for bombs in fighter-bomber version

First Flight Date:
1 June 1939

Operator:
Germany, Turkey

Production:
19 379 (all models)

Right: Focke-Wulf Fw 190A-1 Wk-Nr 0047

Focke-Wulf Fw 190D-9 Germany

Type: single-engined monoplane fighter   **Accommodation:** pilot

Development/History

Developed in 1942 as a replacement for the aborted Fw 190B/C high altitude fighters, the *Langnasen-Dora* (Longnose-Dora) made use of the exceptional inverted inline Junkers Jumo 213 engine, combined with an MW50 water/methanol booster, to achieve an impressive rate of climb and top speed – both crucial ingredients for a Defence of the Reich fighter. In total contrast to the many models and sub-variants of the Fw 190A/G, only the D-9 version of the Dora was produced in large numbers. Service entry was achieved in August 1944, and the first fighters to reach the *Jagdwaffe* were employed as Me 262 airfield defenders. A number of D-9s participated in the last ditch *Bodenplatte* operation staged at dawn on New Year's Day against numerous Allied airfields in western Europe, and the survivors of this mission were later absorbed within the Defence of the Reich force. In February 1945 production commenced on the D-12, which was equipped with an uprated Jumo 213 F-1 engine, a 30 mm cannon firing through the nose and better protective armour for the pilot, but only a handful were built before Germany surrendered in May 1945.

Specification

Dimensions:
Length: 33 ft 5.25 in (10.19 m)
Wingspan: 34 ft 5.5 in (10.50 m)
Height: 11 ft 0.25 in (3.36 m)

Weights:
Empty: 7964 lb (3612 kg)
Max T/O: 10 670 lb (4840 kg)

Performance:
Max Speed: 426 mph (685 kmh)
Range: 520 miles (837 km)
Powerplant: Junkers Jumo 213A-1 (with MW50 water/methanol boost)
Output: 2240 hp (1670 kW)

Armament:
two 13 mm machine guns in nose, two 20 mm cannon in wings; one 1100 lb (500 kg) bomb under fuselage

First Flight Date:
March 1942

Operator:
Germany

Production:
674

Right: Captured Focke-Wulf Fw 190D-9 FE-121 was photographed soon after the end of World War 2

Focke-Wulf Ta 152 Germany

Type: single-engined monoplane fighter

Accommodation: pilot

Development/History

Undoubtedly the ultimate piston-engined German fighter to attain series production in World War 2, the Ta 152 was also the final extrapolation of the Fw 190 family first devised by Dr Kurt Tank in the late 1930s. The Ta 152 was the result of the Luftwaffe's desperate need for faster fighters with a better performance at altitude, and the initial development stages of the aircraft (A- and B-models) saw the Jumo 213 engine combined with a pressurised cockpit and new wing centre section, married to the outer wings and lengthened rear fuselage of an Fw 190A-8. The Ta 152C introduced the boosted Daimler-Benz DB 603LA into the airframe, but only a handful had been built when the definitive Ta 152H was unveiled, fitted again with the Jumo 213E and a drastically increased wingspan. Production commenced in November 1944, and a handful of aircraft were issued to Service Trials units in early 1945. Those that did see action were involved mainly in protecting Me 262 bases, rather than performing their designed role of high altitude USAAF heavy bomber interceptors. Around 170 Ta 152H-1s had been built by the

Specification

Dimensions:
Length: 35 ft 1.5 in (10.71 m)
Wingspan: 47 ft 4.5 in (14.44 m)
Height: 11 ft 1 in (3.38 m)

Weights:
Empty: 8887 lb (4031 kg)
Max T/O: 11 502 lb (5217 kg)

Performance:
Max Speed: 465 mph (748 kmh)
Range: 1250 miles (2011 km) with external tanks
Powerplant: Junkers Jumo 213A-1 (with MW50 water/methanol boost)
Output: 2050 hp (1529 kW)

Armament:
one 30 mm cannon in propeller hub and two 20 mm cannon in wings

First Flight Date:
November 1944

Operator:
Germany

Production:
approximately 200

time the Cottbus factory was captured by invading Soviet forces in the early spring of 1945.

Right: Focke-Wulf Ta 152C-0 R 11 V7

Focke-Wulf Ta 154 Germany

Type: twin-engined monoplane fighter

Accommodation: pilot and radar operator

Development/History

Dubbed 'Moskito' by the Germans due to its wooden construction, the Ta 154 enjoyed far less success than its British namesake. Built of wood in an effort to preserve strategic materials, the Ta 154 was designed in response to a 1942 requirement issued by the Luftwaffe for a specialised night and all-weather fighter. An initial order of 250 was placed in November 1943, and various woodworking firms in eastern Germany and Poland were contracted to work on the 'Moskito'. With a planned maximum production rate of 500 aircraft per month, the Ta 154 had all the appearances of being a serious weapon in the *Nachtjagd* arsenal, as it took the fight to RAF's Bomber Command over Germany. However, the disintegration of the first and second production Ta 154A-1 during a high speed pre-delivery run cast doubts over the quality of manufacture, and the project was immediately halted. A subsequent investigation found that acid levels in the glue used to bond the wood was too high, weakening the joints. Officials decided that it would take too long to find a 'fix' to this problem, so the Ta 154 was

Specification

Dimensions:
Length: 41 ft 3 in (12.57 m)
Wingspan: 52 ft 6 in (16.00 m)
Height: 11 ft 10 in (3.61 m)

Weights:
Empty: 13 933 lb (6320 kg)
Max T/O: 19 842 lb (9000 kg)

Performance:
Max Speed: 399 mph (642 kmh)
Range: 1156 miles (1860 km) with external tanks
Powerplants: two Junkers Jumo 213E engines
Output: 3500 hp (2610 kW)

Armament:
two 30 mm cannon and two 20 mm cannon in the nose

First Flight Date:
7 July 1943

Operator:
Germany

Production:
approximately 75

cancelled. A handful did see limited combat with two frontline nightfighter *gruppe* in late 1944, however.

Right: Focke-Wulf Ta 154 V7

Fokker D.XXI The Netherlands

Type: single-engined monoplane fighter   **Accommodation:** pilot

Development/History

The last single-engined fighter to carry the famous name of Fokker, the D.XXI was a modest fixed undercarriage monoplane fighter that was effectively obsolete by the outbreak of World War 2. Built in small numbers, and only used by three air arms, the type nevertheless acquitted itself well in Dutch hands before being totally overwhelmed during the May 1940 *Blitzkrieg* – close to 40 Ju 52 transports and a handful of Bf 109Es were credited to the brave Dutch fighter pilots in five days of conflict, although they too suffered horrific casualties in the process. The first D.XXIs had been ordered to fill a requirement expressed by the Netherlands East Indies Air Service in the mid-1930s, and the first examples entered Dutch service in the Netherlands itself in early 1938. Licence-built examples were also produced concurrently by VL in Finland, and some 90 D.XXIs were delivered. The final foreign user of the Fokker fighter was Denmark, who bought two directly from the Dutch company, and then built a further ten. The Danish D.XXIs saw little action during the German invasion in the spring of 1940, but the Finnish

examples inflicted heavy casualties on Soviet forces for much of World War 2. Indeed, the final Finnish D.XXI was not retired from service until 1951.

Specification (all dimensions and performance data for Mercury-engined D.XXI)

Dimensions:
Length: 26 ft 11 in (8.20 m)
Wingspan: 36 ft 1 in (11.00 m)
Height: 9 ft 8 in (2.95 m)

Weights:
Empty: 3197 lb (1450 kg)
Max T/O: 4519 lb (2050 kg)

Performance:
Max Speed: 286 mph (460 kmh)
Range: 578 miles (930 km)
Powerplant: Bristol Mercury VII/VIII
Output: 830 hp (619 kW)

Armament:
four 7.7 mm or 7.9 mm machine guns in wings, or two 7.9 mm machine guns and two 20 mm cannon in the wings

First Flight Date:
27 March 1936

Operators:
Denmark, Finland, The Netherlands

Production:
246

Right: Fokker D.XXI FD-322 of the Royal Netherlands Air Force

58

Gloster Gladiator UK

Type: single-engined biplane fighter   Accommodation: pilot

Development/History

The ultimate (and final) British biplane fighter of them all, the Gladiator started life as a company private venture, Gloster basing their new SS.37 (as the Gladiator was designated) very much on its predecessor, the Gauntlet. Although equipped with four guns, the design still embraced the 'old' technology of doped fabric over its wood and metal ribbed and stringered fuselage and wings. Following its first flight in September 1934, the Gladiator I was swiftly put into production, with Gloster eventually building 231 examples. It made its service debut in January 1937, and went on to fly with a further 26 RAF fighter squadrons. The later Mk II was fitted with the Bristol Mercury VIIIA engine, and 252 new-build machines were delivered, and a number of Mk Is upgraded to this spec through the fitment of the later powerplant. Sixty arrestor-hooked Sea Gladiators were also delivered to the Royal Navy, plus a further 165 Mk Is and IIs for foreign export customers. A considerable number of Gladiators were still in service when war broke out in September 1939, and although virtually obsolete, they gave a good account of themselves in France, the Middle East, over Malta and in East Africa.

Specification (all dimensions and performance data for Gladiator Mk I)

Dimensions:

Length: 27 ft 5 in (8.36 m)
Wingspan: 32 ft 3 in (9.83 m)
Height: 10 ft 4 in (3.15 m)

Weights:

Empty: 3450 lb (1565 kg)
Max T/O: 4750 lb (2155 kg)

Performance:

Max Speed: 253 mph (407 kmh)
Range: 428 miles (689 km)
Powerplant: Bristol Mercury VIIIA/AS or IX
Output: 840 hp (626 kW)

Armament:

four 0.303 in machine guns in nose and under wings

First Flight Date:

12 September 1934 (SS.37)

Operators:

Belgium, China, Egypt, Eire, Finland, Greece, Iraq, Latvia, Lithuania, Norway, Portugal, South Africa, Sweden, UK

Production:

768

Right: Gloster Gladiator Mk I of the Belgian air force

Gloster Meteor I/III UK

Type: twin-engined jet fighter   **Accommodation:** pilot

Development/History

The first (and only) Allied jet combat design to reach the frontline during World War 2, the Meteor was initially handicapped (in F I form) because its large size and generous wing area had a detrimental effect on the modest power output of its original Welland engines (rated at a combined thrust of just 3400 lb st). However, these very design features came into their own following development work undertaken by Rolls-Royce which resulted in the Meteor being matched up with the far better Derwent series of turbojet engines from the F III onwards. Gloster built 20 F Is from early January 1944, and these were issued to No 616 Sqn six months later. The jet's first taste of action came within weeks of the unit's arrival at RAF Manston, in Kent, when the aircraft's high speed was used to chase down and destroy a total of 13 V1 flying bombs. By the time No 616 Sqn moved to the Continent in early 1945, the unit had replaced its F Is with Derwent-engined F IIIs. These more powerful Meteors were put to effective use in ground-strafing missions in the final weeks of war. Postwar, the Meteor went on to become the RAF's staple dayfighter, plus serve as an effective two-seat trainer and nightfighter. Many were also sold to foreign air forces.

Specification (all dimensions and performance data for Meteor F I)

Dimensions:
Length: 41 ft 3 in (12.57 m)
Wingspan: 43 ft 0 in (13.10 m)
Height: 13 ft 0 in (3.96 m)

Weights:
Empty: 8140 lb (3693 kg)
Max T/O: 13 800 lb (6260 kg)

Performance:
Max Speed: 415 mph (668 kmh)
Range: 1000 miles (1610 km)
Powerplants: two Rolls-Royce Welland I turbojet engines
Output: 3400 lb st (15.24 kN)

Armament:
four 20 mm cannon in nose

First Flight Date:
5 March 1943

Operator:
UK

Production:
230 (Mk I and III only)

Right: Gloster Meteor F III EE457 was later upgraded into an F IV

Grumman F4F Wildcat USA

Type: single-engined monoplane fighter   **Accommodation:** pilot

Development/History

Derived from a biplane design offered in competition to the more modern Brewster F2A Buffalo monoplane, the Wildcat was the result of a study undertaken by Grumman into the feasibility of a single wing naval fighter. Designated the XF4F-2, it lost out to the rival Brewster in the fly-off due to the latter's superior handling qualities. However, Grumman reworked the prototype into the vastly superior XF4F-3 of March 1939, fitting a more powerful Twin Wasp engine with a two-stage supercharger, increasing the fighter's wing span and redesigning its tail surfaces. After flight trials, the Navy ordered 78 F4F-3s, which they christened the Wildcat. Entering service at the end of 1940, the Wildcat proved to be a worthy opponent for the Japanese A6M Zero-sen during the great carrier battles of 1942-43. The aircraft was also a popular addition to the Royal Navy's Fleet Air Arm, who used various marks from 1940 through to VE-Day. By 1943 General Motors (GM) had commenced building F4F-4s, which they redesignated FM-1s. Later that same year GM switched production to the FM-2, which utilised a turbocharged Wright R-1820-56 Cyclone in place of the Twin Wasp.

Specification (all dimensions and performance data for F4F-4)

Dimensions:
Length: 28 ft 9 in (8.76 m)
Wingspan: 38 ft 0 in (11.58 m)
Height: 11 ft 4 in (3.45 m)

Weights:
Empty: 5895 lb (2674 kg)
Max T/O: 7952 lb (3607 kg)

Performance:
Max Speed: 320 mph (515 kmh)
Range: 770 miles (1239 km)
Powerplant: Pratt & Whitney R-1830-76/86 Twin Wasp
Output: 1200 hp (895 kW)

Armament:
six 0.50 in machine guns in wings; provision for two 250 lb (113 kg) bombs under wings

First Flight Date:
2 September 1937

Operators:
UK, USA

Production:
7808

This swap made for a higher top speed and an optimum altitude some 50 per cent greater than that achieved in the FM-1 – by the time production was terminated in August 1945, no fewer than 4467 FM-2s had been built.

Right: US Navy Grumman F4F-3 BuNo 132205

Grumman F6F Hellcat USA

Type: single-engined monoplane fighter   **Accommodation:** pilot

Development/History

The F6F embodied the early lessons learnt by users of Grumman's previous fleet fighter, the F4F Wildcat, in the Pacific, as well as general pointers from the air war in Europe. Following receipt of the US Navy's order for the fighter in June 1941, Grumman modified the 'paper' aircraft by lowering the wing centre section to enable the undercarriage to be wider splayed, fitted more armour-plating around the cockpit to protect the pilot and increased the size of the fighter's ammunition magazines. Less than a year after being ordered, the prototype XF6F-1 made its first flight, and it was soon realised that a more powerful engine was needed to give the fighter a combat edge – a Pratt & Whitney R-2800-10 was duly installed, resulting in the F-1 being redesignated an F-3. The aircraft made its combat debut in August 1943, and from that point on, the question of aerial supremacy in the Pacific was never in doubt. Hellcats served aboard most US Navy's fleet carriers, being credited with the destruction of 4947 aircraft up to VJ-Day. Amazingly, only three major variants were produced – the -3, the improved -5 and the -3N/-5N nightfighters. The Fleet Air Arm was

Specification (all dimensions and performance data for F6F-3)

Dimensions:
Length: 33 ft 4 in (10.16 m)
Wingspan: 42 ft 10 in (13.06 m)
Height: 14 ft 5 in (4.40 m)

Weights:
Empty: 9042 lb (4101 kg)
Max T/O: 13 228 lb (6000 kg)

Performance:
Max Speed: 376 mph (605 kmh)
Range: 1085 miles (1746 km)
Powerplant: Pratt & Whitney R-2800-10W Double Wasp
Output: 2000 hp (1491 kW)

Armament:
six 0.50 in machine guns in wings; provision for six rockets under wings or 2000 lb (907 kg) bombs under centre section

First Flight Date:
26 June 1942

Operators:
UK, USA

Production:
12 275

also a great believer in the Hellcat, procuring almost 1200 between 1943-45. The F6F saw only limited service postwar, quickly being replaced in the fleet by the Bearcat.

Right: Grumman Hellcat I FN376 of the Royal Navy's Fleet Air Arm

Hawker Hurricane UK

Type: single-engined monoplane fighter   **Accommodation:** pilot

Development/History

The Hurricane's arrival in the frontline in December 1937 saw the RAF finally make the jump from biplane to monoplane fighters. The aircraft owed much to Hawker's ultimate biplane design, the Fury, both types being built around an internal 'skeleton' of four wire-braced alloy and steel tube longerons – this structure was renowned for both its simplicity of construction and durability. The Hurricane also benefited from Hawker's long-standing partnership with Rolls-Royce, whose newly developed Merlin I engine proved to be the ideal powerplant. Toting eight .303-in machine guns, and capable of speeds in excess of 300 mph, the Hurricane I was the world's most advanced fighter when issued to the RAF. Although technically eclipsed by the Spitfire come the summer of 1940, Hurricanes nevertheless outnumbered the former type during the Battle of Britain by three to one, and actually downed more Luftwaffe aircraft than the Vickers-Supermarine fighter. Even prior to its 'finest hour', Hurricanes provided the first RAF aces of the war in France during the *Blitzkrieg*. In 1941 the type was used in the Mediterranean and North Africa, before being flung into action in the Far East against the Japanese. It remained in the frontline in the latter theatre until VJ-Day, despite production having ceased in September 1944.

Specification (all dimensions and performance data for Hurricane Mk I)

Dimensions:

Length: 31 ft 5 in (9.58 m)
Wingspan: 40 ft 0 in (12.19 m)
Height: 13 ft 0 in (3.96 m)

Weights:

Empty: 4982 lb (2260 kg)
Max T/O: 7490 lb (3397 kg)

Performance:

Max Speed: 324 mph (521 kmh)
Range: 600 miles (965 km)
Powerplant: Rolls-Royce Merlin II/III
Output: 1030 hp (768 kW)

Armament:

eight 0.303 in machine guns in wings

First Flight Date:

6 November 1935

Operators:

Australia, Belgium, Canada, Eire, Finland, France, India, The Netherlands, Portugal, Romania, South Africa, Turkey, UK, USSR, Yugoslavia

Production:

14 449 (all models)

Right: Hawker Hurricane Mk I L1648, fitted with a wooden two-bladed propeller

Hawker Sea Hurricane UK

Type: single-engined monoplane fighter   Accommodation: pilot

Development/History

Despite the RAF's No 46 Sqn proving that the Hurricane could take-off and land from a carrier during the ill-fated Norwegian campaign of April 1940, the first dedicated Sea Hurricanes did not finally see their first operations until early 1941. Initially developed to counter the threat posed to Atlantic convoys by long-range Fw 200 Condors, 50 'Hurricats' were converted for use from Catapult Armed Merchant Ships, and once launched, they either had to land ashore or ditch into the sea upon the completion of their mission. The pressing need for more modern fighters for the conventional Fleet Air Arm also resulted in a number of ex-RAF aircraft being converted into Sea Hurricane IBs at around the same time, the standard land-based airframe being fitted with a catapult spool and arrestor hook – little other modifications were carried out. Later variants featured the engine and airframe of the Mk I combined with the Mk IIC's cannon armament, whilst the final naval Sea Hurricane (the Mk IIC) was identical to its RAF equivalent, boasting a four cannon wing and Merlin XX engine. Sea Hurricanes equipped 38 Fleet Air Arm units between 1941-44, and saw action

over the Mediterranean and the Arctic Sea from the decks of fleet and escort carriers, as well as from land bases on Malta and along the North African coast.

Specification (all dimensions and performance data for Sea Hurricane Mk IIC)

Dimensions:
Length: 32 ft 3 in (9.83 m)
Wingspan: 40 ft 0 in (12.19 m)
Height: 13 ft 3 in (4.04 m)

Weights:
Empty: 5800 lb (2631 kg)
Max T/O: 7800 lb (3538 kg)

Performance:
Max Speed: 322 mph (518 kmh)
Range: 460 miles (740 km)
Powerplant: Rolls-Royce Merlin XX
Output: 1460 hp (1089 kW)

Armament:
four 20 mm cannon in wings

First Flight Date:
early 1941

Operators:
Canada, UK

Production:
approximately 800 converted from standard Hurricanes

Right: Hawker Sea Hurricane Mk IB aboard the escort carrier HMS Argus in September 1943

70

Hawker Typhoon UK

Type: single-engined monoplane fighter   **Accommodation:** pilot

Development/History

The Typhoon was the first fighter to enter RAF service capable of achieving speeds in excess of 400 mph in level flight. However, the brutish Hawker fighter was almost deemed a failure right at the start of its career when the combination of poor climb and altitude performance, unreliability of its new Napier Sabre (chosen in favour of the cancelled Rolls-Royce Vultee/Hawker Tornado combination) and suspect rear fuselage assembly cast serious doubts over its suitability for frontline service. Refusing to give up on the design, Hawker and Napier spent over a year (from mid-1941 through to mid-1942) 'beefing up' the airframe and correcting engine maladies to the point where the Typhoon was found to be an excellent low altitude fighter – it effectively blunted the Luftwaffe's Fw 190 'hit and run' raiders, who frequently terrorised the south coast of England in 1942-43. Its proven ability at low-level also made it the ideal platform for the ground attack mission, its quartet of 20 mm cannon and deadly array of rockets and bombs allowing Typhoon pilots to roam the skies over occupied western Europe attacking all manner of targets from ships to tanks. One of the key weapons in the Allied arsenal for Operation *Overlord*, the RAF possessed some 26 Typhoon squadrons by mid 1944. The last Typhoon was delivered to the RAF in November 1945.

Specification (all dimensions and performance data for Typhoon Mk IB)

Dimensions:
Length: 31 ft 11 in (9.73 m)
Wingspan: 41 ft 7 in (12.67 m)
Height: 15 ft 3.5 in (4.66 m)

Weights:
Empty: 9800 lb (4445 kg)
Max T/O: 13 980 lb (6341 kg)

Performance:
Max Speed: 405 mph (652 kmh)
Range: 980 miles (1577 km) with external tanks
Powerplant: Napier Sabre IIA
Output: 2180 hp (1626 kW)

Armament:
four 20 mm cannon in wings; provision for two 500 lb (227 kg) or 1000 lb (454 kg) bombs or eight 3 in/60 lb (7.62 cm/27 kg) rockets under wings

First Flight Date:
24 February 1940

Operators:
Canada, New Zealand, UK

Production:
3330

Right: Hawker Typhoon Mk IB

72

Hawker Tempest V UK

Type: single-engined monoplane fighter   **Accommodation:** pilot

Development/History

Based closely on the Typhoon, the Tempest was actually designated the Typhoon II early on in its development phase. The most obvious difference between the two designs was the adoption of a thin, elliptical, laminar flow, wing on the Tempest, which replaced the thick chord flying surface of the earlier design – the 'thick' wing created serious compressibility problems for the Typhoon at high speeds throughout its career. Due to the fitment of the new 'thin' wing, the fuel tanks previously housed in the wings had to moved into the fuselage, resulting in the latter being lengthened by two feet. A dorsal fin was also added to the fuselage. Although several versions of the Tempest were planned by Hawker, only the Sabre-engined Mk V was completed in time to see service with the RAF prior to war's end. The first production standard aircraft flew in June 1943, and the first operational wing was formed in April 1944, and VE-Day, 11 squadrons within Fighter Command were equipped with Tempest Vs. Early aircraft suffered from engine reliability problems caused by overspeeding propellers, but once this was rectified, the Tempest continued the Typhoon's tradition in the low-

level fighter-bomber role. Unlike its predecessor, the Tempest also proved to be effective at medium to high altitudes too, and aside from downing 638 V1s, it was also credited with the destruction of 20 Me 262s. Postwar, the Mk V was supplanted by the Bristol Centaurus-engined Tempest II.

Specification

Dimensions:
Length: 33 ft 8 in (10.26 m)
Wingspan: 41 ft 0 in (12.50 m)
Height: 16 ft 1 in (4.90 m)

Weights:
Empty: 9250 lb (4196 kg)
Max T/O: 13 640 lb (6187 kg)

Performance:
Max Speed: 416 mph (669 kmh)
Range: 1530 miles (2462 km) with external tanks
Powerplant: Napier Sabre IIA
Output: 2180 hp (1626 kW)

Armament:
four 20 mm cannon in wings; provision for two 1000 lb (454 kg) bombs or eight 3 in/60 lb (7.62 cm/27 kg) rockets under wings

First Flight Date:
2 September 1942

Operators:
New Zealand, UK

Production:
805 (Mk V only)

Right: Hawker
Tempest Mk V JN729

Heinkel He 219 Germany

Type: twin-engined monoplane fighter   **Accommodation:** pilot and radar operator

Development/History

Arguably the ultimate German piston-engined nightfighter to attain series production, the *Uhu* ('Owl') was fitted with the deadly combination of advanced airborne radar and fearsome cannon armament – the latter including the oblique, upward-firing, *Schräge Musik* (literally 'slanted music') 30 mm cannon installation in the rear fuselage of the large fighter. Developed privately by Heinkel independent of any official interest from the Luftwaffe, the significance of the He 219 became apparent as RAF Bomber Command increased its volume of raids on Germany in 1941-42. The prototype *Uhu* immediately impressed with its speed and manoeuvrability in the wake of its first flight in November 1942, and by May 1943 a special trials unit had started flying pre-production He 219A-0s in combat from a base in Holland. During the first six sorties flown by the Heinkel, some 20 bombers were destroyed, including six previously elusive Mosquitos. Full production A-2s began reaching frontline units by early 1944, and the *Uhu* soon developed into a specialist Mosquito 'destroyer'. Just when it looked like the *Nachtjagd* was at last on the verge of receiving a dedicated nightfighter, rather than a converted day fighter or bomber, production of the He 219A-7 was terminated in May 1944 by senior Luftwaffe personnel in favour of the unsuccessful Ta 154 and Ju 388J. Rapidly reinstated following the failure of the latter types, He 219 production never recovered from this setback.

Specification (all dimensions and performance data for He 219A-7)

Dimensions:
Length: 50 ft 11.75 in (15.54 m)
Wingspan: 60 ft 8 in (18.49 m)
Height: 13 ft 5.5 in (4.10 m)

Weights:
Empty: 24 692 lb (11 200 kg)
Max T/O: 33 730 lb (15 300 kg)

Performance:
Max Speed: 416 mph (669 kmh)
Range: 1243 miles (2000 km)
Powerplants: two Daimler-Benz DB 603E engines
Output: 3800 hp (2834 kW)

Armament:
two 30 mm cannon in wing roots, two 30 mm and two 20 mm cannon in ventral tray, two upward-firing 30 mm cannon in rear fuselage

First Flight Date:
15 November 1942

Operator:
Germany

Production:
294

Right: Heinkel He 219A-7 FE612 is seen in Allied hands after VE-Day

Heinkel He 162 Germany

Type: single-engined monoplane jet fighter

Accommodation: pilot

Development/History

Developed as the *Volksjäger* ('People's Fighter') by Heinkel in the final desperate months of Nazi Germany, the He 162 was designed, built and flown in the staggeringly short time of just ten weeks between October and December 1944. Of mixed construction (wooden wings, metal fuselage and metal/wood tailplane), the He 162 was powered by a BMW 003 turbojet perched atop the fuselage. Simple to construct, the fighter was slated for production by three factories, whose combined output amounted to no fewer than 4000 He 162s a month! Faced with a shortage of pilots to fly these jets, the Luftwaffe was told to crew the aircraft with hastily trained members of the Hitler Youth – fortunately the war ended before this flawed plan could be put into place. Ten prototypes were built by Heinkel before the definitive production standard was settled on, the He 162A-1 featuring 30 mm cannon, anhedral wingtips and an increased span tailplane. The A-1 proved to have a short-lived production life, however, for it suffered badly from cannon vibration whenever the weapons were fired, so it was replaced by the A-2 version, which featured 20 mm cannon instead. The He 162A

Specification

Dimensions:
Length: 29 ft 8.5 in (9.05 m)
Wingspan: 23 ft 7.25 in (7.21 m)
Height: 8 ft 6 in (2.59 m)

Weights:
Empty: 4796 lb (2175 kg)
Max T/O: 5940 lb (2694 kg)

Performance:
Max Speed: 490 mph (788 kmh)
Range: 410 miles (660 km)
Powerplant: BMW 003E-1/2
Output: 1764 lb st (7.9 kN)

Armament:
two 30 mm or two 20 mm cannon in the nose

First Flight Date:
6 December 1944

Operator:
Germany

Production:
approximately 150 officially accepted by the Luftwaffe

officially entered service with I./JG 1 at Leck in January 1945, but Allied aircraft recorded few encounters with the fighter prior to VE-Day.

Right: Heinkel He 162A-2 T-2-489 was brought to the USA postwar

I.A.R.80/81 Romania

Type: single-engined monoplane fighter

Accommodation: pilot

Development/History

This indigenous fighter was developed in the late 1930s by Industria Aeronautica Romania (I.A.R.) to replace the Polish P.Z.L. P.24E, which had been built under licence by I.A.R. Numerous features of the Polish fighter were incorporated into the design of the I.A.R.80, including the fitting of a fixed tail skid rather than a tailwheel. The first production of 51 I.A.R.80s appeared in the spring of 1940, and these early aircraft featured an enclosed cockpit and a cantilever tailplane. Issued to Romanian air force units in January 1941, they were subsequently joined by 80 A-, 30 B- and 50 C-model I.A.R.80s, each of which featured the more powerful I.A.R-K 14-1000A radial engine and a variety of machine gun and cannon armament. The follow-on I.A.R.81 family was closely modelled on the I.A.R.80 airframe, but with added structural strengthening to allow the aircraft to perform fighter-bomber and dive-bomber roles. The first of these entered service in October 1941, and A- B- and C-model sub-variants again boasted varying gun and bomb fits. The last I.A.R.81 was produced in late 1943, after which the factory concentrated on local production

of the Bf 109G-6. The I.A.R.80/81 made its combat debut on the Eastern Front in 1941/42, before returning to Romania to perform home defence missions over Bucharest and the Ploesti oilfields. Surviving examples were converted into two-seat I.A.R.80DC trainers postwar, and remained in service until 1952.

Specification (all dimensions and performance data for I.A.R.81C)

Dimensions:
Length: 29 ft 5.15 in (8.97 m)
Wingspan: 34 ft 6.15 in (10.52 m)
Height: 11 ft 9.75 in (3.60 m)

Weights:
Empty: 4685 lb (2125 kg)
Max T/O: 6768 lb (3070 kg)

Performance:
Max Speed: 337 mph (542 kmh)
Range: 640 miles (1030 km) with external tanks
Powerplant: I.A.R-K 14-1000A
Output: 1025 hp (764 kW)

Armament:
four 7.92 mm machine guns and two 20 mm cannon in wings

First Flight Date:
April 1939 (I.A.R.80)

Operator:
Romania

Production:
461

Right: This I.A.R.81C wears late-war Romanian roundels

Junkers Ju 88C/G/R Germany

Type: twin-engined monoplane fighter

Accommodation: three-/four-man crew

Development/History

Although designed first and foremost for the fast medium bomber role, Junkers' superbly versatile Ju 88 was easily modified into a *Zerstörer* heavy fighter, and the first such aircraft flew as early as 1939. The primary changes carried out to the basic A-model airframe by Junkers centred on the replacement of the former's glazed nose with a solid fairing (equipped with both cannon and machine guns) and the modification of the aircraft's bomb bay to house a weapons gondola. The evolution of the C-model heavy fighter mirrored that of the Ju 88 bomber, with more powerful engines, greater span wings and strengthened fuselage being incorporated into the *Zerstörer* as it appeared on the A-model. A small number of Ju 88Cs made the type's combat debut over Poland in September 1939, and from then on heavy fighter variants saw action on every front up to VE-Day. The ultimate Ju 88 fighter variant was the G-model of 1944, which boasted a FuG 220 or 227 radar, an astounding array of cannon and machine gun armament and advanced Junkers Jumo (methanol-water injected) or BMW engines. A dedicated nightfighter, the first Ju 88G-1s

entered service with the *Nachtjagd* in the summer of 1944, replacing Ju 88C/Rs as well as some Bf 110Gs. Despite suffering heavy losses in the final months of the war, those *Nachtjagdgeschwader* equipped with Ju 88Gs also inflicted serious casualties on Bomber Command right up to VE-Day.

Specification (all dimensions and performance data for Ju 88G-7)

Dimensions:

Length: 54 ft 1.5 in (16.50 m)
Wingspan: 65 ft 10.5 in (20.08 m)
Height: 15 ft 11 in (4.85 m)

Weights:

Normal loaded: 28 900 lb (13 109 kg)
Max T/O: 32 350 lb (14 674 kg)

Performance:

Max Speed: 389 mph (626 kmh)
Range: 1400 miles (2253 km)
Powerplants: two Junkers Jumo 213E engines
Output: 3450 hp (2572 kW)

Armament:

four 20 mm cannon in ventral tray, one 13 mm machine gun in rear cockpit and two upward-firing 20 mm cannon in upper fuselage

First Flight Date:

21 December 1936 (Ju 88A)

Operator:

Germany

Production:

approximately 6000 Ju 88C/G/Rs

Right: Junkers Ju 88G-1

Kawanishi N1K1 Kyofu Japan

Type: single-engined monoplane floatplane fighter

Accommodation: pilot

Development/History

Built to fulfil an Imperial Japanese Navy (IJN) requirement for a single-seat fighter floatplane issued in September 1940, the Kyofu was unquestionably the most advanced aircraft of its type to see combat during World War 2. Indeed, despite having to cope with the incredible drag created by its central float and outriggers, the fighter's laminar flow wing and powerful Mitsubishi radial engine gave the N1K1 a startling performance. Designed to protect marauding Japanese amphibious assault forces from attacking fighters, by the time the Kyofu entered pre-production testing in early 1943, the tide of war had already turned, and it was tasked with a defensive rather than an offensive role. In July of that same year the first production N1K1 began to leave the Kawanishi factory, and these were sent to Netherlands East Indies and Borneo. Less than 100 had been built when production ended in March 1944, and the survivors were pooled on Lake Biwa, on the island of Honshu, in 1945. From there they flew home defence sorties, as the American assault on Japan reached its climax.

Specification

Dimensions:
Length: 34 ft 9 in (10.59 m)
Wingspan: 39 ft 4.5 in (12.00 m)
Height: 15 ft 7 in (4.75 m)

Weights:
Empty: 6067 lb (2752 kg)
Max T/O: 8183 lb (3712 kg)

Performance:
Max Speed: 304 mph (489 kmh)
Range: 1036 miles (1667 km)
Powerplant: Mitsubishi MK4C Kasai 13 of MK4E Kasai 15
Output: 1460 hp (1089 kW) and 1530 hp (1141 kW) respectively

Armament:
two 7.7 mm machine guns in nose and two 20 mm cannon in wings

First Flight Date:
6 May 1942

Operator:
Japan

Production:
97

Allied codename: 'Rex'

Right: Kawanishi N1K1 Kyofu pre-production aircraft

Kawanishi N1K1-J Shiden Japan

Type: single-engined monoplane fighter   **Accommodation:** pilot

Development/History

Privately developed by Kawanishi from their Kyofu floatplane fighter, the Shiden retained the N1K1's basic airframe in combination with a retractable wheeled undercarriage. Aside from the fitment of the latter, the primary changes made centred on a switch of powerplants from a Mitsubishi to a Nakajima radial and the shifting of the wing to mid-fuselage position. The adoption of the mid-wing would later cause many problems with the aircraft's overly long (and weak) undercarriage legs, and complex retraction system. Initial flight trials of the Shiden revealed not only the undercarriage problems, but also that the fighter was some 45 mph slower than anticipated due to the Homare engine failing to deliver its promised levels of power. Pilots also complained of restricted visibility due to the positioning of the wing mid-fuselage. Despite these failings, the N1K1-J was still a vast improvement on the IJN's venerable A6M and temperamental J2M, and when the first Shidens saw combat over the Philippines in October 1944, Allied pilots soon learnt to respect its fighting abilities. Aside from the N1K1-J/-Ja fighter variants, the fighter-bomber optimised N1K1-Jb/-Jc also saw action in the ill-fated home defence campaign of 1945.

Specification

Dimensions:
Length: 29 ft 2 in (8.89 m)
Wingspan: 39 ft 4.5 in (12.00 m)
Height: 13 ft 4 in (4.06 m)

Weights:
Empty: 6387 lb (2897 kg)
Max T/O: 9526 lb (4321 kg)

Performance:
Max Speed: 363 mph (584 kmh)
Range: 1581 miles (2544 km) with external tanks
Powerplant: Nakajima NK9H Homare 21
Output: 1990 hp (1484 kW)

Armament:
two 7.7 mm machine guns in nose, two 20 mm cannon in wings, plus some aircraft fitted with additional 20 mm cannon in underwing gondolas

First Flight Date:
6 December 1942

Operator:
Japan

Production:
1007

Allied codename: 'George'

Right: Kawanishi N1K1-J Shiden

Kawanishi N1K2-J Shiden-KAI Japan

Type: single-engined monoplane fighter   **Accommodation:** pilot

Development/History

Acknowledging the faults of the N1K1-J even before the latter had entered series production, Kawanishi commenced work on the improved N1K2-J in mid-1943. To eradicate the undercarriage problems, the wing on the Shiden-KAI was lowered to a similar position to that employed by the Kyofu floatplane. Other improvements saw the engine moved forward and the fuselage slightly lengthened to cure a centre of gravity problem, redesigned tail surfaces and a revised cowling shape. The construction of the fighter was also simplified, allowing building man hours to be reduced and the overall weight of the aircraft to be reduced by 500 lbs. Deliveries of aircraft to the frontline commenced in July 1944, and eight factories were tooled up for mass-production of the N1K1-2, but B-29 raids severely hampered overall output to the extent that just 428 had been built by VJ-Day – one factory even failed to produce a single completed fighter. The Shiden-KAI was easily the best IJN fighter of the war, and could more than hold its own against any Allied foe, including the much-feared F4U-4 Corsair. The handful of sentai that received the N1K2-J were employed almost exclusively on home defence operations.

Specification

Dimensions:
Length: 30 ft 8 in (9.35 m)
Wingspan: 39 ft 4.5 in (12.00 m)
Height: 13 ft 0 in (3.96 m)

Weights:
Empty: 5858 lb (2657 kg)
Max T/O: 10 714 lb (4860 kg)

Performance:
Max Speed: 369 mph (594 kmh)
Range: 1488 miles (2395 km) with external tanks
Powerplant: Nakajima NK9H Homare 21
Output: 1990 hp (1484 kW)

Armament:
four 20 mm cannon in wings; four 551 lb (250 kg) bombs

First Flight Date:
31 December 1943

Operator:
Japan

Production:
428

Allied codename: 'George 21'

Right: Kawanishi N1K2-J Shiden-KAI

Kawasaki Ki-45-KAI Toryu Japan

Type: twin-engined monoplane fighter

Accommodation: pilot and observer/gunner

Development/History

Designed in 1937 as the Japanese Army Air Force's first twin-engined fighter, the Ki-45 proved to be a successful platform for both the ground attack and nightfighting missions come World War 2. The prototype aircraft was initially powered by licence-built Bristol Mercury engines, but these provided such a disappointing performance that they were replaced by Nakajima Ha-25 radials. Kawasaki also thoroughly overhauled the design at around the same time, the revised fighter, designated Ki-45-KAI (for *kaizo* – modified), emerging with a remodelled fuselage, revised wings and tail, heavier armament and increased fuel capacity. By October/November 1942 the first production standard Ki-45-KAIas had made their combat debuts over Burma and China, respectively. Employed as a ground attack platform using a variety of weaponry, the Ki-45 also eventually became a makeshift, 'radarless' nightfighter following the shifting of B-24 raids by the USAAF's Fifth Air Force to the hours of darkness. Further specialist cannon and machine gun fits were trialled and approved by the nightfighting Ki-45 sentais, which were in turn adopted by Kawasaki. New engines were also mated to the Ki-45 in late 1943, resulting in the production of the near-definitive Toryu, the Ki-45-KAI-Hei (or KAIc). This aircraft proved to be a formidable opponent for the B-29 when it appeared over the home islands in 1945, for it was able to perform interceptions both during the day and at night, at any altitude.

Specification (all dimensions and performance data for Ki-45-KAI-Hei)

Dimensions:
Length: 36 ft 1 in (11.00 m)
Wingspan: 49 ft 3.25 in (15.00 m)
Height: 12 ft 1.75 in (3.70 m)

Weights:
Empty: 8146 lb (3695 kg)
Max T/O: 11 631 lb (5276 kg)

Performance:
Max Speed: 340 mph (547 kmh)
Range: 1243 miles (2000 km)
Powerplants: two Mitsubishi Ha-102 engines
Output: 2160 hp (1610 kW)

Armament:
one 37 mm cannon in ventral tunnel, two upward-firing 20 mm cannon behind forward cockpit, and one 7.92 mm machine gun in rear cockpit

First Flight Date:
May 1941

Operator: Japan

Production: 1701

Allied codename: 'Nick'

Right: Kawasaki Ki-45-KAI-Hei Toryu of the 53rd Sentai

Kawasaki Ki-61 Hein Japan

Type: single-engined monoplane fighter **Accommodation:** pilot

Development/History

One of the few examples of Axis material co-operation bearing fruition in World War 2, the Kawasaki Ha-40 inline engine was a lightened development of the excellent Daimler-Benz DB 601A inverted V12 inline engine. The fighter designed specially to utilise this powerplant was the sleek Ki-61 Hein which, aside from having an inline rather than a more traditional radial engine, also boasted a high wing loading, armour protection for the pilot and self-sealing tanks – all things rarely associated with Japanese combat aircraft of the period. The Ki-61 made its combat debut over the jungles of New Guinea in April 1943, and it quickly proved itself to be more than a match for Allied P-38s, P-39s and P-40s. In production until war's end, the K-61 was the subject of many improvements, both in respect to its armament (which was increased through the fitment of cannon and bomb racks) and the power output of its Kawasaki engine. The resulting K-61-II-KAI had a performance to rival any piston-engined contemporaries, especially at altitude, but it in turn suffered from serious engine reliability maladies that were never solved. Production of the II-KAI

commenced in September 1944, but the combination of powerplant problems and a devastating B-29 raid on the Kawasaki engine works meant that only 99 of the 374 airframes completed received the definitive Ha-140 V12. The remainder were either destroyed on the ground or completed as Ki-100s.

Specification (all dimensions and performance data for Ki-61-I)

Dimensions:
Length: 28 ft 8.5 in (8.75 m)
Wingspan: 39 ft 4.5 in (12.00 m)
Height: 12 ft 2 in (3.71 m)

Weights:
Empty: 4872 lb (2210 kg)
Max T/O: 7165 lb (3250 kg)

Performance:
Max Speed: 368 mph (592 kmh)
Range: 684 miles (1100 km)
Powerplant: Kawasaki Ha-40
Output: 1175 hp (876 kW)

Armament:
two 12.7 mm machine guns in nose and two in wings (Ki-61-I only)

First Flight Date:
December 1941

Operator: Japan

Production:
3078 (275 engineless examples completed as Ki-100s)

Allied codename: 'Tony'

Right: Kawasaki Ki-61-I Hein of the 37th Sentai

Kawasaki Ki-100 Japan

Type: single-engined monoplane fighter   **Accommodation:** pilot

Development/History

Considered by many to be Japan's best fighter of the war, the Ki-100 was born out of an urgent need for a fighter that could intercept USAAF B-29s raiding the home islands at altitudes of around 30,000 ft. Originally the Ki-61-II-KAI had been slated to fill this requirement, but chronic problems with its inline Ha-140 powerplant resulted in over 200 airframes sat idle on the ground devoid of an engine. In November 1944 Kawasaki was ordered by the Japanese Ministry of Munitions to install a replacement engine, and after some searching, the Mitsubishi Ha-112 radial was chosen. Engineers studied the engine mountings of an imported Fw 190A to see how their German counterparts had mated a 'fat' radial to a slim fuselage. Armed with this knowledge, work proceeded swiftly on the Ki-100-I, and 271 airframes were fitted with the Mitsubishi engine between March and June 1945. The new fighter came as an unpleasant surprise to the Americans, with the fighter immediately enjoying success not only against the feared B-29s, but also Hellcats, Mustangs and Corsairs. Aside from being a joy to fly, the Ki-100 also proved immensely popular with

long-suffering groundcrews – many of whom had been struggling with the Ha-40/-140 for longer than they cared to remember. Finally, an all-new version of the Ki-100 entered production in May 1945, the -Ib featuring cut-down rear fuselage decking and an all-round vision canopy.

Specification (all dimensions and performance data for Ki-100-I)

Dimensions:
Length: 28 ft 11.25 in (8.82 m)
Wingspan: 39 ft 4.5 in (12.00 m)
Height: 12 ft 3.5 in (3.75 m)

Weights:
Empty: 5567 lb (2525 kg)
Max T/O: 7705 lb (3495 kg)

Performance:
Max Speed: 360 mph (579 kmh)
Range: 1367 miles (2200 km) with external tanks
Powerplant: Mitsubishi Ha-112-II
Output: 1500 hp (1118 kW)

Armament:
two 20 mm cannon in nose and two 12.7 mm machine guns in wings; provision for two 551 lb (250 kg) bombs under wings

First Flight Date:
1 February 1945

Operator:
Japan

Production:
396

Allied codename: no name given

Right: Kawasaki Ki-100-I of the 5th Sentai

94

Lavochkin LaGG-3 USSR

Type: single-engined monoplane fighter   Accommodation: pilot

Development/History

Built primarily of wood, the LaGG-3 can trace its origins to the I-22 fighter of 1938-39, which was subsequently designated the LaGG-1 in honour of the principal design bureau involved – Lavochkin, Gorbunov and Gudkov. Early flight trials revealed serious performance and handling deficiencies, so fixed (later automatic) wing slats, new outer wing panels, aerodynamic revisions and additional fuel tanks were added. The overall structure of the fighter – redesignated I-301 – was lightened and its armament also increased. After further flight tests, the LaGG-1 was ordered into production in late 1940, and with the fitment of the more powerful M-105PF engine, the fighter entered service as the LaGG-3 in early 1941. No further airframe or engine changes were subsequently made to the LaGG-3 for the remainder of its brief production life, but variations in armament were common. The aircraft proved easy to build, and by the time the last LaGG-3 left the factory in June 1942, some 6527 had been built in less than two years. The most modern fighter in the Soviet arsenal at the time of the German invasion, the LaGG-3 earned a reputation for rugged reliability, although it was not a match for the Luftwaffe fighters of the day, being underpowered and less manoeuvrable than either the Bf 109F/G or the Fw 190A – both exacted a heavy toll on the LaGG-3.

Specification

Dimensions:
Length: 29 ft 2.5 in (8.90 m)
Wingspan: 32 ft 2 in (9.80 m)
Height: 8 ft 10 in (2.69 m)

Weights:
Empty: 5776 lb (2620 kg)
Max T/O: 7231 lb (3280 kg)

Performance:
Max Speed: 348 mph (560 kmh)
Range: 497 miles (800 km)
Powerplant: Klimov M-105PF
Output: 1240 hp (925 kW)

Armament:
one 20 mm or 23 mm cannon in propeller hub and two 7.62 mm or 12.7 mm machine guns in upper cowling; some with two 12.7 mm machine guns under wings; provision for 441 lb (200 kg) bomb load or six 82 mm rockets under wings

First Flight Date:
30 March 1940

Operator:
Finland, USSR

Production:
6527

Right: Lavochkin LaGG-3, captured by the Japanese

Lavochkin La-5/-7 USSR

Type: single-engined monoplane fighter   Accommodation: pilot

Development/History

Reports of the LaGG-3's inadequacies in combat against Luftwaffe (and Finnish) fighters resulted in the aircraft's inline M-105PF being replaced by the far more powerful Shvetsov M-82 radial in early 1942. Testing soon proved that the modified fighter was not only appreciably faster than its predecessor, but also far more capable at medium to high altitudes. Designated the Lavochkin La-5, the first examples to reach the frontline (during the battle for Stalingrad in late 1942) were actually re-engined LaGG-3s. Aside from the change of engine, the aircraft had also had its machine gun armament replaced by two 20 mm cannon. By late March 1943 production of the definitive La-5N had commenced, this variant featuring a fuel-injected M-82FN for better performance at altitude and cut down rear fuselage decking and a new canopy for better all round vision. The La-5FN was more than a match for the Bf 109G, and could hold its own with the Fw 190. In November 1943 the further improved La-7 started flight trials, this model boasting even greater performance thanks to the lightening of its overall structure and adoption of the metal wing spars featured in late-build La-5FNs. Attention was also paid to reducing the fighter's drag coefficient, which resulted in the adoption of a revised cowling and inboard wing leading edge surfaces. The La-7 entered service in the spring of 1944, and went on to become the favoured mount of most Soviet aces.

Specification (all dimensions and performance data for La-7)

Dimensions:
Length: 29 ft 2.5 in (8.90 m)
Wingspan: 32 ft 1.75 in (9.80 m)
Height: 8 ft 6.25 in (2.60 m)

Weights:
Empty: 5842 lb (2620 kg)
Max T/O: 7496 lb (3400 kg)

Performance:
Max Speed: 423 mph (680 kmh)
Range: 615 miles (990 km)
Powerplant: Shvetsov M-82FN
Output: 1850 hp (1380 kW)

Armament:
two or three 20 mm cannon in upper cowling; provision bombs or rockets under wings

First Flight Date:
March 1942 (La-5)

Operator:
Czechoslovakia, USSR

Production:
9920 La-5s and 5753 La-7s

Right: Lavochkin La -7

Lockheed P-38 Lightning USA

Type: twin-engined fighter   Accommodation: pilot

Development/History

The P-38 Lightning was Lockheed's first venture into the world of high performance military aircraft. Keen to break into the lucrative military marketplace, the company had eagerly responded to the USAAC's 1937 Request for Proposals pertaining to the acquisition of a long-range interceptor. Aside from its novel twin-boom and central nacelle layout, the prototype XP-38, as it was designated by Lockheed, utilised butt-joined and flush-riveted all-metal skins (and flying surfaces) – a first for a US fighter. The XP-38's test programme progressed well, and aside from some minor adjustments to the flying surfaces and introduction of progressively more powerful Allison engines, frontline P-38s differed little from the prototype throughout the aircraft's six-year production run. The appellation 'Lightning' was bestowed upon the P-38 by the RAF when the type was ordered in 1940, and duly adopted by the Americans the following year. In the event the RAF was so disappointed in the performance of the unsupercharged aircraft it received in 1941 that their order for 667 was cancelled – the supercharger fitted to the V-1710 engine was still designated a

classified item by the US government at this point in the war, and thus restricted from overseas sale. However, the definitive P-38 models – namely the E, F, H, J and L – fitted *with* supercharged engines, improved Fowler flaps and extra fuel, proved more than a match for Axis fighters across the globe.

Specification (all dimensions and performance data for P-38J)

Dimensions:
Length: 37 ft 10 in (11.53 m)
Wingspan: 52 ft 0 in (15.85 m)
Height: 9 ft 10 in (3.00 m)

Weights:
Empty: 12 780 lb (5797 kg)
Max T/O: 21 600 lb (9798 kg)

Performance:
Max Speed: 414 mph (666 kmh)
Range: 2260 miles (3637 km) with external tanks
Powerplants: two Allison V-1710-89/-91 engines
Output: 2850 hp (2126 kW)

Armament:
one 20 mm cannon and four 0.50 in machine guns in nose; maximum bomb load 4000 lb (1814 kg) under wings

First Flight Date:
27 January 1939

Operator:
USA

Production:
10 036 (including photo-recce variants)

Right: Lockheed P-38J-10 Lightning

Macchi C.200 Saetta Italy

Type: single-engined fighter   **Accommodation:** pilot

Development/History

Like the majority of Italian fighter aircraft of World War 2, the C.200 was a joy for its pilots to fly, possessing excellent manoeuvrability and positive handling qualities. However, like its contemporaries, the Macchi was woefully under-armed by the standards of the day, being fitted with just two 12.7 mm machine guns. The Saetta entered service with the *Regia Aeronautica* in October 1939, and by the time Italy entered the war in June of the following year, some 156 had been delivered. The first 240 C.200s were delivered with fully enclosed canopies, although this feature was quickly deleted when pilots complained of poor ventilation and restricted vision. Aside from this modification, the Saetta remained essentially unchanged throughout its production career, with the adoption of additional wing guns (under development for the follow-on C.202 Folgore) for later-build aircraft being the only other change incorporated by Macchi. In the field, numerous C.200s were adapted to carry underwing bombs or fuel tanks, and these fighters were redesignated C.200CBs. The Saetta first saw action over Malta in 1940, and was subsequently involved in combat over the

Eastern Front, North Africa, the Western Desert, Greece, Sicily and Yugoslavia. Like most surviving Italian combat aircraft, the C.200 went on to see further service with both the pro-Allied Co-Belligerent Air Force and the pro-German *Aeronautica Nazionale Repubblicana* following Italy's surrender in September 1943. Indeed, it remained in limited production until 1944.

Specification

Dimensions:
Length: 26 ft 10.5 in (8.19 m)
Wingspan: 34 ft 8.5 in (10.58 m)
Height: 11 ft 6 in (3.50 m)

Weights:
Empty: 4451 lb (2019 kg)
Max T/O: 5710 lb (2590 kg)

Performance:
Max Speed: 312 mph (502 kmh)
Range: 540 miles (870 km)
Powerplant: Fiat A.74 RC38
Output: 870 hp (649 kW)

Armament:
two 12.7 mm machine guns in nose; later aircraft additional two 7.7 mm machine guns in wings; C.200CB, guns and 705 lb (320 kg) bomb load under wings

First Flight Date:
24 December 1937

Operator:
Italy

Production:
1153

Right: Macchi C.200 Saetta

Macchi C.202 Folgore Italy

Type: single-engined fighter   **Accommodation:** pilot

Development/History

Whilst the C.200 had been a solid, reliable fighter, it had always suffered from a lack of straightline speed. To solve this problem, Macchi turned away from home-grown radial engines for the Saetta's replacement, and instead chose to use Daimler-Benz's excellent DB 601A inline engine as proven in the Bf 109E. The resulting fighter was 60 mph faster than the C.200, possessed a superior rate of climb and could cruise at altitudes in excess of 37,500 ft. Designated the C.202, initial production aircraft reached the frontline in July 1941 fitted with imported German engines, but the remaining 800+ were equipped with the licence-built Alfa Romeo version. Unfortunately for pilots, Macchi once again restricted armament to just two 12.7 mm machine guns, although late-build examples were also fitted with two additional underwing guns – a fighter-bomber variant, designated the C.202CB, was also duly produced, whilst those tropicalised (through the fitment of a sand filter) were known as C.202ASs. The Folgore quickly proved superior to both the Hurricane II and P-40 Tomahawk/Kittyhawk during its first North African engagements, and examples would later see action over in the Balkans, the Western Desert, Sicily, the Eastern Front and Malta. Like the C.200, the Folgore also served in modest numbers on both sides after the Italian surrender, and production of the fighter continued until 1944.

Specification

Dimensions:
Length: 29 ft 0.5 in (8.85 m)
Wingspan: 34 ft 8.5 in (10.58 m)
Height: 9 ft 11.5 in (3.03 m)

Weights:
Empty: 5545 lb (2515 kg)
Max T/O: 6766 lb (3069 kg)

Performance:
Max Speed: 372 mph (598 kmh)
Range: 475 miles (764 km)
Powerplant: Alfa Romeo RA.1000 RC41-1 Monsone (Daimler-Benz DB 601A)
Output: 1175 hp (876 kW)

Armament:
two 12.7 mm machine guns in nose; later aircraft additional two 7.7 mm machine guns in wings, some with two 20 mm cannon under wings; C.202CB, guns and 705 lb (320 kg) bomb load under wings

First Flight Date:
10 August 1940

Operator:
Italy

Production:
approximately 1200

Right: Macchi C.202 Folgore

Macchi C.205V Veltro Italy

Type: single-engined monoplane fighter   **Accommodation:** pilot

Development/History

The final word in the Macchi fighter dynasty, the C.205V again relied on a German engine – DB 605A-1, this time – for its power. The resulting combination produced what many Allied pilots considered to be the best Italian fighter of the war. Despite Macchi's best efforts to streamline production of the Veltro by using the C.200 wing and C.202 fuselage aft of the engine firewall, the unreliable supply of engines and other industrial problems caused by increased Allied bombing delayed the C.205's service entry until mid-1943. Indeed, by the time of Italy's surrender in September of that year, only 177 had been delivered (66 of which were in frontline service). The Veltro had made its combat debut during the ill-fated defence of Sicily and southern Italy, and following the capitulation, roughly 140 aircraft were used by the pro-German *Aeronautica Nazionale Repubblicana* and 25 issued to a Luftwaffe *gruppe* in-theatre. A further 112 C.205Vs were built by Macchi through to May 1944, when persistent Allied air raids finally shut the production line down. The Veltro remained in Italian air force service postwar, and 42 refurbished examples (mostly re-engined C.202s) were subsequently supplied to Egypt in 1948–49, where they saw action against the embryonic Israeli air force.

Specification

Dimensions:
Length: 29 ft 0.5 in (8.85 m)
Wingspan: 34 ft 8.5 in (10.58 m)
Height: 9 ft 10.5 in (3.00 m)

Weights:
Empty: 5690 lb (2581 kg)
Max T/O: 7513 lb (3408 kg)

Performance:
Max Speed: 399 mph (642 kmh)
Range: 590 miles (950 km)
Powerplant: Fiat RA.1050 RC58 Tifone
(Daimler-Benz DB 605A-1)
Output: 1475 hp (1100 kW)

Armament:
two 12.7 mm machine guns in nose, two 7.7 mm machine guns in wings or two 20 mm cannon under wings; 705 lb (320 kg) bomb load under wings

First Flight Date:
19 April 1942

Operators:
Germany, Italy

Production:
291

Right: Macchi C.205V Veltro

Messerschmitt Bf 109E Germany

Type: single-engined monoplane fighter   **Accommodation:** pilot

Development/History

Designed to meet a 1934 *Reichluftfahrtministerium* (RLM) requirement for a single-seat monoplane fighter, the original Bf 109 V1 was the winning competitor in a 'fly off' that involved three other designs from proven German aviation companies. Light and small, the first production-standard Bf 109s (B-1 models) to enter service in early 1937 proved their worth during the Spanish Civil War. By the time Germany invaded Poland in September 1939, the re-engined Bf 109E was rolling off the Messerschmitt production line in great quantity, the now-familiar airframe being paired up with the powerful Daimler-Benz DB 601. This combination had been tested as long ago as June 1937, when a pre-production aircraft had been flown with a carburetted DB 600 fitted in place of the D-model's Junkers Jumo 210Da, but the subsequent availability of the Bf 109E had been hampered by delays in the development of the appreciably more powerful Daimler-Benz engine. However, these problems had been sorted out by early 1939. Built in huge numbers, and in a great array of sub-variants for the fighter, reconnaissance, fighter-bomber and shipboard fighter roles, the Bf 109E proved

to be the master of all its European contemporaries bar the Spitfire Mk I/II, to which it was considered an equal. Aside from fighting over Poland, the E-model saw combat throughout the *Blitzkrieg* of 1940 and then the Battle of Britain which followed, in the Balkans in 1941 and in the opening phases of the North African and Soviet campaigns.

Specification (all dimensions and performance data for Bf 109E-3)

Dimensions:

Length: 28 ft 0 in (8.55 m)
Wingspan: 32 ft 4.5 in (9.87 m)
Height: 8 ft 2 in (2.49 m)

Weights:

Empty: 4189 lb (1900 kg)
Max T/O: 5875 lb (2665 kg)

Performance:

Max Speed: 348 mph (560 kmh)
Range: 410 miles (660 km)
Powerplant: Daimler-Benz DB 601Aa
Output: 1175 hp (876 kW)

Armament:

two 7.9 mm machine guns in upper cowling, two 20 mm cannon in wings; some E-3s additional 20 mm cannon in propeller hub; fighter-bomber variant provision for carriage of one 551 lb (250 kg) bomb under fuselage

First Flight Date:

June 1937 (Bf 109 V10)

Operators:

Bulgaria, Croatia, Germany, Romania, Slovakia, Spain, Switzerland, Yugoslavia

Production: approximately 4000

Right: Messerschmitt Bf 109E-4 Wk-Nr 1361

Messerschmitt Bf 109F Germany

Type: single-engined monoplane fighter   **Accommodation:** pilot

Development/History

Developed in response to the availability of uprated DB 201N/E engines, the Bf 109F also exhibited much aerodynamic reworking in comparison with the Bf 109E. The engine cowl was appreciably smoother, the propeller hub enlarged, wing tips rounded off, rudder reduced in size, tailplane struts deleted and the tailwheel made to retract. The ailerons and flaps were also improved and the armament restricted to a single cannon and two machine guns, all of which was nose/engine mounted. The resulting fighter was undoubtedly the best handling Bf 109 of them all – it was also the most aesthetically pleasing of the many variants produced. The first production F-1s entered service on the Channel front in January 1941, and almost immediately revised versions with better armament and more powerful engines were put into production. Although a joy to fly, the F-model was criticised for its lack of armament (particularly when compared with the Bf 109E-3/-4s that they were in the process of replacing), so some units carried out field modifications that saw two 20 mm cannon added in gondolas beneath the wings. The Bf 109F equipped two-thirds of the *Jagdwaffe*

110

Specification (all dimensions and performance data for Bf 109F-4)

Dimensions:
Length: 29 ft 2.5 in (8.90 m)
Wingspan: 32 ft 6.5 in (9.92 m)
Height: 8 ft 6.5 in (2.60 m)

Weights:
Empty: 5259 lb (2390 kg)
Max T/O: 6872 lb (3117 kg)

Performance:
Max Speed: 388 mph (624 kmh)
Range: 528 miles (850 km) with external tank
Powerplant: Daimler-Benz DB 601E-1
Output: 1350 hp (1007 kW)

Armament:
one 20 mm cannon in propeller hub and two 7.9 mm machine guns in upper cowling; F-4B fighter-bomber variant provision for carriage of one 551 lb (250 kg) bomb under fuselage

First Flight Date:
July 1940

Operators:
Croatia, Germany, Hungary, Italy, Spain

Production:
approximately 2200

when the Germans launched their assault on the USSR in June 1941, and the fighter also saw much action in North Africa in 1941-42. However, the introduction of the definitive Bf 109G in the early summer of 1942 resulted in the production of the F-model being immediately halted.

Right: Messerschmitt Bf 109F-3

Messerschmitt Bf 109G/K Germany

Type: single-engined monoplane fighter   Accommodation: pilot

Development/History

The Bf 109G combined the F-model's refined airframe with the larger, heavier and considerably more powerful 1475 hp DB 605 engine to produce the most successful Messerschmitt fighter variant of them all. Cockpit pressurisation was also introduced for the first time with the G-1, although most later sub-variants lacked this feature. Produced in staggering numbers from early 1942 until war's end, some 24,000+ Bf 109G/Ks were constructed in total – including an overwhelming 14,212 in 1944. Numerous modifications to the basic G-1 were introduced either in the factory (as Umrüst-Bausätze factory conversion sets) or in the field (Rüstsätze), and these included provision for extra armament, additional radios, introduction of a wooden tailplane, the fitting of a lengthened tailwheel and the installation of the MW50 water/methanol-boosted DB 605D engine. In an attempt to standardise the equipment of the frontline force, Messerschmitt produced the Bf 109G-6 in late 1942, and this model included many of these previously ad hoc additions. Unfortunately, the continual addition of weighty items like wing cannon and larger engines to the once slight airframe of the Bf 109 eliminated

much of the fighter's manoeuvrability, and instead served to emphasise the aircraft's poor low speed performance, lateral control and ground handling. The final variant to enter widespread service with the Luftwaffe was the Bf 109K-4, which incorporated all the best parts of the G-series sub-types (which went up to the G-14), including the improved vision hood, extended tailplane and tailwheel, and DB 605DCM engine.

Specification (all dimensions and performance data for Bf 109G-6)

Dimensions:
Length: 29 ft 7.5 in (9.03 m)
Wingspan: 32 ft 6.5 in (9.92 m)
Height: 8 ft 2.5 in (2.50 m)

Weights:
Empty: 5893 lb (2673 kg)
Max T/O: 7496 lb (3400 kg)

Performance:
Max Speed: 386 mph (621 kmh)
Range: 620 miles (998 km) with external tank
Powerplant: Daimler-Benz DB 605AM
Output: 1800 hp (1342 kW)

Armament:
one 20 mm cannon in propeller hub and two 13 mm machine guns in upper cowling, two 20 mm cannon under wings; provision for various underfuselage and underwing stores

First Flight Date: late summer 1941

Operators:
Bulgaria, Croatia, Finland, Germany, Hungary, Italy, Romania, Slovakia, Switzerland

Production:
approximately 23 500 G-models and around 750 K-models

Right:
Messerschmitt
Bf 109G-6 Wk-
Nr 412951

Messerschmitt Bf 110 Germany

Type: twin-engined monoplane fighter   **Accommodation:** two-/three-man crew

Development/History

Designed in 1934-35 to fill the perceived need for a high-speed, long-range, heavily-armed twin-engined fighter, Messerschmitt's Bf 110 *Zerstörer* (destroyer) fulfilled all these criterion. Seen as the ultimate bomber escort, capable of sweeping the sky clean of enemy fighters, the Bf 110 relied more on its firepower than manoeuvrability to survive in combat. Too late to see action in the Spanish Civil War, the Bf 110C made the aircraft's combat debut over Poland, where it dominated the skies in an environment of overwhelming Luftwaffe air superiority. These successes continued throughout the 'Phoney War' and into the early days of the *Blitzkrieg* in the west, but come the Battle of Britain, serious flaws in the *Zerstörer* concept were graphically exposed. Following the loss of over 200 Bf 110s during the campaign, the day fighter role was given over almost exclusively to the single-seat *gruppe*, and the Messerschmitt 'twin' sent to operate either on less hostile fronts like the Balkans and in the Mediterranean, or in the rapidly developing nightfighter role. The latter mission was ideally suited to a big fighter like the Bf 110, and by 1943, the dedicated, radar-equipped, G-model accounted for around 60 per cent of the overall *Nachtjagd* force. The most effective nightfighter variant was the G-4, which boasted DB 605B-1 engines, FuG 212 Lichtenstein C-1, SN-2 or 221a radar and various cannon fits, depending on the sub-type. So effective was the Bf 110G in this nocturnal role, that the fighter remained in production until March 1945.

Specification (all dimensions and performance data for Bf 110C-4)

Dimensions:
Length: 39 ft 8.5 in (12.10 m)
Wingspan: 53 ft 4.75 in (16.27 m)
Height: 11 ft 6 in (3.50 m)

Weights:
Empty: 9920 lb (4500 kg)
Normal loaded: 15 300 lb (6940 kg)

Performance:
Max Speed: 349 mph (561 kmh)
Range: 565 miles (909 km)
Powerplants: two Daimler-Benz DB 601A-1 engines
Output: 2200 hp (1640 kW)

Armament:
two 20 mm cannon and four 7.9 mm machine guns in nose cowling, 7.9 mm machine gun in rear cockpit; C-4/B fighter-bomber variant, maximum load of 1102 lb (500 kg) bombs carried externally; C-7, maximum load of 2205 lb (1000 kg) bombs

First Flight Date: 12 May 1936

Operator:
Germany

Production:
approximately 6050

Right:
Messerschmitt
Bf 110C-1

Messerschmitt Me 262 Germany

Type: twin-engined jet monoplane fighter

Accommodation: single-seat fighter-bomber or two-seat nightfighter

Development/History

The world's very first operational jet fighter, the Me 262 was also the most advanced aircraft of its generation to actually see combat. Design work on the Messerschmitt commenced as early as 1938, and the first (of five) tailwheeled prototype, fitted with a nose-mounted Junkers Jumo 210 piston engine, completed its maiden flight on 4 April 1941. Unfortunately for Messerschmitt, work on the aircraft's revolutionary turbojet powerplants failed to keep pace with their development of the airframe, and it was not until 18 July 1942 that the first successful flight was made with the preferred Junkers Jumo 003 turbojets installed – the BMW 003 had initially been trialled, but persistent failures had seen it discarded in early 1942. With the engine/airframe combination at last sorted out, political interference from no less a figure than the Führer himself saw the programme side-tracked for a number of months as he insisted that the aircraft be developed as a bomber. Sense finally prevailed in early 1944, and the first aircraft to reach the frontline saw combat in June of that same year. Despite Germany being bombed virtually 24 hours a day during the final 12 months of

Specification (all dimensions and performance data for Me 262A-1a)

Dimensions:

Length: 34 ft 9.5 in (10.60 m)
Wingspan: 41 ft 0.5 in (12.51 m)
Height: 11 ft 6.75 in (3.83 m)

Weights:

Empty: 9742 lb (4420 kg)
Normal loaded: 14 101 lb (6396 kg)

Performance:

Max Speed: 540 mph (870 kmh)
Range: 652 miles (1050 km)
Powerplants: two Junkers Jumo 004B-1/-2 or -3 turbojet engines
Output: 3960 lb st (17.8 kN)

Armament:

A-1a, four 30 mm cannon in nose; A-2a, cannon, plus 1102 lb (500 kg) external bombs; A-1a/U1, four 30 mm and two 20 mm cannon; A-1b, cannon, bombs and provision for 24 underwing rockets

First Flight Date:

18 July 1942 (first all jet-powered flight)

Operator:

Germany

Production:

1433

the war, 1400+ Me 262s were completed by Messerschmitt, and a further 500 were lost in air raids. Engine reliability, fuel shortages and unrealistic operational taskings restricted the frontline force to around 200 jets at any one time, but these nevertheless accounted for over 200 Allied aircraft during day and night interceptions.

Right: Messerschmitt Me 262A-1a of Kommando Nowotny

Messerschmitt Me 163B Komet Germany

Type: single-engined rocket monoplane fighter

Accommodation: pilot

Development/History

The only rocket-powered fighter to see combat in World War 2, the very high performance Me 163B was developed by Dr Alexander Lippisch from his pre-war series of tailless gliders. The first rocket-powered aircraft to be flown was the DFS 194, which carried a series of very short flights in 1940. By this time Dr Lippisch and his team had come under the control of Messerschmitt, and this partnership resulted in the Me 163A, which achieved a top speed of 624 mph during trials staged in the summer of 1941. Messerschmitt drastically revised the design to produce the frontline capable Me 163B in early 1943, and after lengthy delays waiting for a reliable HWK 509 rocket motor to become available, the prototype completed its first flight on 23 June. The Walter engine was capable of outstanding performance, but ran for just eight minutes. To achieve the previously unheard of 15,950 ft per minute rate of climb (the Me 262 could achieve 3937 ft per minute), the Me 163B relied on a volatile fuel combination of T-stoff (hydrogen-peroxide and water) and C-stoff (hydrazine hydrate and methyl alcohol). In order to save weight, Messerschmitt dispensed with a fixed undercarriage, choosing instead to launch the aircraft via a jettisonable trolley and then rely on the pilot's skill to land using a fixed skid. Just one *gruppe* was equipped with the aircraft, making its combat debut in August 1944.

Specification

Dimensions:
Length: 19 ft 2.25 in (5.85 m)
Wingspan: 30 ft 7.25 in (9.33 m)
Height: 9 ft 1 in (2.77 m)

Weights:
Empty: 4206 lb (4420 kg)
Normal loaded: 9502 lb (4310 kg)

Performance:
Max Speed: 593 mph (954 kmh)
Range: maximum powered endurance of 8 minutes
Powerplant: Walter HWK 509-A2
Output: 3750 lb st (16.8 kN)

Armament:
two 30 mm cannon in wing roots

First Flight Date:
23 June 1943 (Me 163B)

Operator:
Germany

Production:
approximately 355 Me 163Bs

Right: Messerschmitt Me 163B-1a of 2./JG 400

Mikoyan-Gurevich MiG-1/-3 USSR

Type: single-engined monoplane fighter   **Accommodation:** pilot

Development/History

Created by ex-Polikarpov designers Ivanovic ('Ayrtom') Mikoyan and Mikhail Gurevich, the MiG-1/-3 family of fighters was built to satisfy a Soviet Air Force requirement for just such an aircraft. Established in 1939, the company flew the first of three prototype MiG-1s on 5 April 1940, and despite the fighter (of mixed steel tube and wooden construction) exhibiting several unenviable handling characteristics, it was approved for limited production. In an effort to eradicate as many of these problems as possible, MiG swiftly reworked their design and came up with the MiG-3, which solved almost all of the handling woes. It benefited from having had its engine repositioned further forward, the dihedral on its outer wing panels increased, the fuselage decking reduced to help aid all-round vision, better armour protection fitted, boosted fuel capacity, and its structure physically strengthened and simplified to ease construction. Despite all these modifications, the MiG-3 actually entered frontline service just weeks after the MiG-1 in April 1941. Despite the MiG-3 reputedly being the world's fastest fighter then in production, the aircraft suffered badly in the first months of war

between Germany and the USSR, as most aerial engagements were fought at low level, where the aircraft's manoeuvrability and armament were found to be lacking. Designed as a high altitude fighter, surviving MiG-3s were switched to ground attack and armed reconnaissance work, before being totally replaced in the frontline in early 1943.

Specification (all dimensions and performance data for MiG-3)

Dimensions:
Length: 26 ft 9 in (8.15 m)
Wingspan: 33 ft 9.5 in (10.30 m)
Height: 8 ft 8 in (2.64 m)

Weights:
Empty: 5952 lb (2602 kg)
Normal loaded: 7385 lb (3350 kg)

Performance:
Max Speed: 398 mph (640 kmh)
Range: 510 miles (820 km)
Powerplant: Mikulin AM-35A
Output: 1350 hp (1007 kW)

Armament:
one 12.7 mm and two 7.62 mm machine guns in nose, two 12.7 machine guns under or in wings; maximum bomb load of 485 lb (220 kg) bombs or six 82 mm rockets under wings

First Flight Date:
5 April 1940 (MiG-1)

Operator:
USSR

Production:
approximately 100 MiG-1s and 3120 MiG-3s

Right: Mikoyan-Gurevich MiG-3s

Mitsubishi A5M   Japan

Type: single-engined monoplane fighter   **Accommodation:** pilot

Development/History

The first monoplane fighter built for the IJN, the Mitsubishi A5M proved to be a very popular mount with its pilots in the latter half of the 1930s, perfectly bridging the gap between the biplane fighters of the past and the high performance A6M Zero of World War 2. Crucial in securing air superiority over the forces tasked with invading China and Manchuria during the Sino-Japanese War of 1937-40, the first A5M1s had entered service on the eve of the conflict starting. A version of the fighter was also offered to the Japanese Army Air Force, but the latter's obsession with highly manoeuvrable designs resulted in Nakajima's Ki-27 being chosen instead. Re-engined and aerodynamically 'cleaned up' in the late 1930s, the A5M4 was the final production version of the 'Claude'. Entering service in 1938, the aircraft was capable of carrying an external fuel tank or small bombs. Mitsubishi's production of the A5M4 ceased in 1940, but a small number continued to be built by satellite factories until 1942. The 'Claude' was still very much a frontline fighter in December 1941, and examples participated in several early battles, including the invasion of the Philippines. Replaced by the vastly superior Zero in 1942, the A5M lingered on in the single- and dual-seat fighter training role until the final examples were destroyed during the Kamikaze attacks of 1944-45.

Specification (all dimensions and performance data for A5M4)

Dimensions:
Length: 24 ft 9.75 in (7.56 m)
Wingspan: 36 ft 1 in (11.00 m)
Height: 10 ft 8.75 in (3.27 m)

Weights:
Empty: 2784 lb (1263 kg)
Max T/O: 4017 lb (1822 kg)

Performance:
Max Speed: 270 mph (434 kmh)
Range: 746 miles (1200 km) with external tanks
Powerplant: Kotobuki 41 KAI
Output: 785 hp (585 kW)

Armament:
two 7.7 mm machine guns in nose; provision for two underwing 66 lb (30 kg) bombs

First Flight Date:
4 April 1935

Operator:
Japan

Production:
1094

Allied codename: 'Claude'

Right: Mitsubishi A5M4

Mitsubishi A6M2/3 Zero Japan

Type: single-engined monoplane fighter   Accommodation: pilot

Development/History

Undoubtedly the most famous Japanese combat aircraft of World War 2, the A6M was developed by Mitsubishi to meet a demanding IJN requirement for a replacement to the successful A5M of the late 1930s. Officially designated the Navy Type 0 Carrier Fighter *Reisen* ('Zero Fighter'), the A6M offered an impressive mix of high performance, long range and superb manoeuvrability, all in a lightweight and modestly powered airframe. The first two prototype A6M1s were powered by the relatively underpowered and undeveloped Mitsubishi Zuisei 13 engine, and a switch was soon made to the Sakae, which it retained until war's end. Redesignated the A6M2, the first production standard Model 11s were delivered to the IJN in July 1940, and barely two months later the variant saw action over China when 13 Zeros tangled with 27 Polikarpov I-15s and I-16s and shot them all down without suffering a single loss! Production switched to the Model 21 at around the same time, this variant having folding wingtips for deck elevator compatibility. A6M2s made up no less than two-thirds of the IJN's fighter force by 7 December 1941, and 135 Zeros took part in the

Specification (all dimensions and performance data for A6M2 Model 21)

Dimensions:
Length: 29 ft 8.75 in (9.06 m)
Wingspan: 39 ft 4.5 in (12.00 m)
Height: 10 ft 0.15 in (3.05 m)

Weights:
Empty: 3704 lb (1680 kg)
Max T/O: 6164 lb (2796 kg)

Performance:
Max Speed: 331 mph (533 kmh)
Range: 1930 miles (3105 km) with external tanks
Powerplant: Nakajima NK1C Sakae 12
Output: 950 hp (708 kW)

Armament:
two 7.7 mm machine guns in nose, two 20 mm cannon in wings; provision for two underwing 132 lb (60 kg) bombs

First Flight Date:
1 April 1939

Operator: Japan

Production: 4335

Allied codename: 'Zeke' (A6M2) and 'Hap'/'Hamp' and 'Zeke 32' (A6M3)

Pearl Harbor assault. By then the re-engined A6M3 was just entering production, the new variant being powered by a supercharged Sakae 21 rated at 1130 hp (843 kW). This variant also dispensed with the folding wingtips, leaving the wings with a 'squared off' appearance. A6M3 production finally ended in mid-1943.

Right: This Mitsubishi A6M2 Model 21 was captured by American forces in 1942

Mitsubishi A6M5/7 Zero Japan

Type: single-engined monoplane fighter   **Accommodation:** pilot

Development/History

The most produced of all Zero variants, the A6M5 was initially developed by Mitsubishi as a 'stop gap' fighter until the follow-on A7M Reppu was cleared for production. However, terminal delays with the later fighter, and problems with the land-based J2M Raiden, resulted in the A6M5 remaining in production until war's end. Retaining the airframe, powerplant and armament of the A6M3, the 'new' Zero was, however, fitted with modified flaps and ailerons and thickened wing skinning to allow pilots to attain greater terminal speeds whilst attempting to dive away from Allied fighters. The A6M3 reached the frontline in October 1943, and by March 1944 the first sub-variants were rolling off the production line. Modifications included even thicker wing skinning, improved ammunition feed for the wing and nose guns, and armour protection for the pilot and fuel tanks. All these additions added weight to the Zero, which was still powered by the modestly uprated Sakai 21. By now thoroughly out-classed by the US Navy and Army Air Force fighters in-theatre, hundreds of A6M5s were lost during the battles of 1944-45. In an attempt to redress the balance, Mitsubishi mated a water/methanol injected Sakai 31 with an A6M5 Model 52c to produce the A6M7 Model 63. Limited production commenced in May 1945, but only 150 had been completed by VJ-Day.

Specification (all dimensions and performance data for A6M7 Model 63)

Dimensions:
Length: 29 ft 11 in (9.12 m)
Wingspan: 36 ft 1 in (11.00 m)
Height: 11 ft 6 in (3.50 m)

Weights:
Empty: 4136 lb (1876 kg)
Loaded weight: 6025 lb (2733 kg)

Performance:
Max Speed: 340 mph (548 kmh)
Range: 945 miles (1520 km)
Powerplant: Nakajima Sakae 31
Output: 1130 hp (843 kW)

Armament:
two 20 mm cannon and two 13 mm machine guns in wings, one 13 mm machine gun in the nose; provision for one 551 lb (250 kg) bomb under fuselage

First Flight Date:
August 1943 (A6M5)

Operator:
Japan

Production:
approximately 6000 A6M5s and 150 A6M7s

Allied codename: 'Zeke'

Right: Mitsubishi A6M7 in Japanese surrender markings

Mitsubishi J2M Raiden Japan

Type: single-engined monoplane fighter   **Accommodation:** pilot

Development/History

Built as a land-based naval interceptor optimised for speed and rate of climb, rather than manoeuvrability, the J2M was potentially an outstanding fighter that remained plagued by technical problems and industrial upheaval throughout its brief production life. Initial development work started in October 1938, but Mitsubishi's technical emphasis was firmly honed on the A6M, which was also in its embryonic stages at that point. When work on the J2M was finally given the go ahead in early 1941, engineers soon got bogged down with problems associated with the cooling system for the Kasei 13 engine, as well as technical snags associated with the laminar flow wing. A change of engines to the Kasei 23a did little to improve reliability, and by March 1943, only 11 production J2M2s had been delivered to the IJN. Once in service, the Raiden suffered several accidents due to jammed controls, and by the time this had been sorted out in early 1944, less than 150 J2Ms had been built. The J2M3 was introduced into service soon after this, and limited production of this variant allowed several sentai to re-equip with the Raiden. Although never available in the numbers hoped for by the IJN, the J2M nevertheless proved to be a capable home defence fighter in the final year of the war.

Specification (all dimensions and performance data for J2M3)

Dimensions:
Length: 32 ft 7.5 in (9.94 m)
Wingspan: 35 ft 5.25 in (10.80 m)
Height: 12 ft 11.25 in (3.94 m)

Weights:
Empty: 5423 lb (2460 kg)
Loaded weight: 7573 lb (3435 kg)

Performance:
Max Speed: 363 mph (584 kmh)
Range: 655-1180 miles (1054-1900 km)
Powerplant: Mitsubishi MK4A-R Kasei 23a
Output: 1800 hp (1342 kW)

Armament:
four 20 mm cannon in wings; provision for two 132 lb (60 kg) bombs under wings

First Flight Date:
20 March 1942

Operator:
Japan

Production:
476 by Mitsubishi and small quantity by Koza Naval Air Arsenal

Allied codename: 'Jack'

Right: Two Mitsubishi J2M3 Raidens of the Allied Technical Air Intelligence Unit, South-East Asia in early 1946

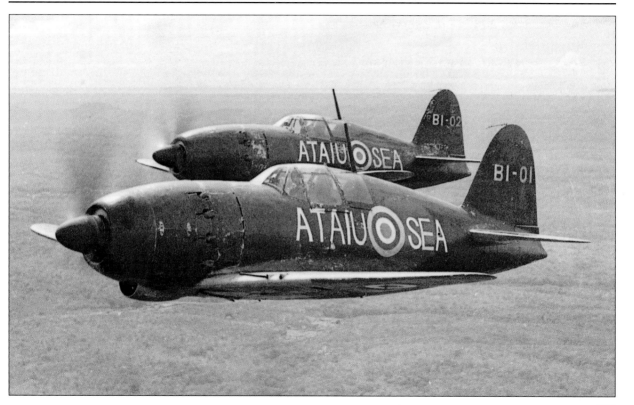

Morane-Saulnier MS 406 France

Type: single-engined monoplane fighter   **Accommodation:** pilot

Development/History

The *Armée de l'Air*'s staple fighter at the outbreak of World War 2, the MS 406 was effectively outclassed by opposing German fighters in respect to both its performance and armament. These deficiencies resulted in over 400 being lost during the Battle of France, with MS 406 pilots in turn claiming 175 victories. Developed from the MS 405, which had in turn been built by Morane-Saulnier in response to a requirement issued by the *Armée de l'Air* for a modern *monoplane de chasse*, 1000 MS 406s were hastily ordered in March 1938 when the French government grew alarmed at the Nazi annexations of Czechoslovakia and Austria. Of mixed construction (conventional steel tube framing and fabric for the fuselage, but with the rest of the structure covered in Plymax – plywood skinning bonded to metal alloy), the first production aircraft reached the frontline in late 1938. A number of MS 406s were also sold to anxious European air forces in the final 18 months of peace, with Finland and Turkey both buying substantial quantities, and Poland being on the cusp of receiving the first of no fewer than 160 fighters when it was invaded by Germany. Following the surrender of France

in June 1940, surviving MS 406s were operated not only by the Vichy French, but also by the Luftwaffe as well, whilst other surplus examples were sent to Croatia, Finland and Italy.

Specification

Dimensions:
Length: 26 ft 9.25 in (8.16 m)
Wingspan: 34 ft 9.75 in (10.61 m)
Height: 9 ft 3.75 in (2.84 m)

Weights:
Empty: 4189 lb (1900 kg)
Max T/O: 6000 lb (2722 kg)

Performance:
Max Speed: 302 mph (486 kmh)
Range: 466 miles (750 km)
Powerplant: Hispano-Suiza 12Y-31
Output: 860 hp (641 kW)

Armament:
one 20 mm cannon firing through propeller hub and two 7.5 mm machine guns in wings

First Flight Date:
8 August 1935 (MS 405)

Operators:
Croatia, Finland, France, Germany, Italy, Switzerland, Turkey

Production:
17 MS 405, 1077 MS 406 and 84 Swiss-built D-3800

Right: Morane-Saulnier MS 406

Nakajima Ki-27 Japan

Type: single-engined monoplane fighter   **Accommodation:** pilot

Development/History

Winner of a 1935 competition held by the *Koku Hombu* (Air Headquarters of the Imperial Army) to find a monoplane fighter, the Nakajima PE defeated rival designs from Mitsubishi and Kawasaki due to its outstanding manoeuvrability. The very similar Ki-27 evolved from the PE within months of the latter's first flight, and following the construction of ten pre-production airframes boasting longer span wings, the first definitive K-27as rolled out of the factory in early 1938. Little changed throughout its service life, the first 'Nates' were issued to units involved in the Sino-Japanese War on March of 1938, and these fighters soon secured total control of the skies for the Japanese forces. In May of 1939, the Ki-27 also proved more than a match for superior numbers of Soviet fighters encountered during the Nomonhan Incident along the Manchukuo/Outer Mongolian border. Army pilots claimed no fewer than 1340 aircraft destroyed during the four-month-long campaign, although postwar research has pruned the actual loss figure to around 200. Upon the outbreak of the Pacific War, the Ki-27 equipped all but two frontline Army sentai,

132

and the type supported the invasions of the Philippines, Burma, the Netherlands East Indies and Malaya, although it had been all but replaced by the Ki-43 by the end of 1942. Relegated to fighter training duties, a number of Ki-27s survived to become platforms for kamikaze attacks in the last months of the war.

Specification

Dimensions:

Length: 24 ft 8.5 in (7.53 m)
Wingspan: 37 ft 1.25 in (11.31 m)
Height: 10 ft 8 in (3.25 m)

Weights:

Empty: 2447 lb (1110 kg)
Loaded weight: 3946 lb (1790 kg)

Performance:

Max Speed: 292 mph (470 kmh)
Range: 1060 miles (1705 km) with external tanks
Powerplant: Nakajima Ha-1b
Output: 780 hp (582 kW)

Armament:

two 7.7 mm machine guns in nose; provision for four 55 lb (25 kg) bombs externally

First Flight Date:

15 October 1936

Operators:

Japan, Manchuria, Thailand

Production:

3399

Allied codename: 'Nate'

Right: Nakajima Ki-27-Otsu of the Akeno Fighter School in 1942

Nakajima Ki-43 Hayabusa Japan

Type: single-engined monoplane fighter **Accommodation:** pilot

Development/History

The staple Japanese Army Air Force (JAAF) fighter of World War 2, the Ki-43 was produced in greater numbers than any of its land-based contemporaries. Developed as a direct replacement for the Ki-27, the Hayabusa (Peregrine) embraced the same design philosophy as the 'Nate' in that it was built to be supremely manoeuvrable at the expense of effective armament, protection for the pilot and structural strength. Following the delivery of ten service trials aircraft in 1939-40 (which were criticised by JAAF test pilots for not being as agile as the Ki-27), production Ki-43-Is began to arrive in the frontline in the spring of 1941. Three sub-variants of the two-bladed -I were produced between April 1941 and February 1943, all of which featured varying armament. The 'Oscar' made its combat debut in the opening phase of the Japanese invasion of South-East Asia, and flying alongside the more numerous Ki-27, it swiftly cleared the skies of any Allied opposition. Despite these early successes, pilots complained that the Ki-43-I was underpowered, so Nakajima answered these claims with the re-engined Ki-43-II of late 1942. Aside from the fitment of the

supercharged Ha-115 radial engine, the new fighter also employed a three-bladed constant speed propeller. The -II also had reduced-span 'clipped' wings, strengthened underwing hardpoints, limited pilot armour and a revised windscreen and canopy. Although thoroughly outclassed even after the Ki-43-II/III had arrived in the frontline, the 'Oscar' remained a key asset in the JAAF arsenal through to VJ-Day.

Specification (all dimensions and performance data for Ki-43-IIb)

Dimensions:
Length: 29 ft 3.25 in (8.92 m)
Wingspan: 35 ft 6.75 in (10.84 m)
Height: 10 ft 8.75 in (3.27 m)

Weights:
Empty: 4211 lb (1910 kg)
Max T/O: 6450 lb (2926 kg)

Performance:
Max Speed: 329 mph (529 kmh)
Range: 1095 miles (1762 km) with external tanks
Powerplant: Nakajima Ha-115
Output: 1150 hp (857 kW)

Armament:
two 12.7 mm machine guns in nose; provision for two 551 lb (250 kg) bombs externally

First Flight Date:
January 1939

Operators:
Japan, Thailand

Production:
5919

Allied codename: 'Oscar'

Right: Nakajima Ki-43-II Hayabusa of the 2nd Chutai/25th Sentai

Nakajima Ki-44 Shoki *Japan*

Type: single-engined monoplane fighter   **Accommodation:** pilot

Development/History

Comparable to the Mitsubishi J2M in its design concept, the Ki-44 sacrificed manoeuvrability and lightness of flying controls for sheer straight-line speed and rate of climb. As a result of these characteristics, the aircraft was initially unpopular with pilots, but once the JAAF became involved in intercepting American heavy bomber formations at medium to high altitudes in 1943-44, the Shoki (Devil-Queller) came into its own. Nevertheless, its high landing speed and difficult handling characteristics remained a problem throughout its career, and many were written off in operational accidents. Indeed, spins, stalls and snap rolls were all banned in the Ki-44. Production Shokis started to reach the frontline in early 1942, the type making its combat debut over the jungles of China-Burma-India (CBI). Later that same year the -I was replaced in production by the -II, which featured a more powerful Ha-109 engine, improved armament and pilot and fuel tank protection. Aside from its service over the CBI, the Ki-44 also saw action over Malaya, in defence of the oilfields at Palembang, on Sumatra, and over the home islands. Production of the Ki-44 ended in

Specification (all dimensions and performance data for Ki-44-II)

Dimensions:
Length: 28 ft 10 in (8.79 m)
Wingspan: 31 ft 0 in (9.45 m)
Height: 10 ft 8 in (3.25 m)

Weights:
Empty: 4643 lb (2106 kg)
Max T/O: 6598 lb (2993 kg)

Performance:
Max Speed: 376 mph (605 kmh)
Range: 1056 miles (1700 km) with external tanks
Powerplant: Nakajima Ha-109
Output: 1520 hp (1133 kW)

Armament:
Ki-43-II, two 7.7 mm machine guns in nose and two 12.7 mm machine guns in wings

First Flight Date:
August 1940

Operator:
Japan

Production:
1225

Allied codename: 'Tojo'

December 1944 to allow Nakajima to concentrate its efforts on the vastly superior Ki-84 Hayate.

Right: The third prototype Nakajima Ki-44-II Shoki

Nakajima J1N1 Gekko Japan

Type: twin-engined monoplane fighter   **Accommodation:** two-/three-man crew

Development/History

Although originally developed in 1938 as a shore-based long-range fighter for the IJN, by the time the J1N entered service in August 1942, the concept of a twin-engined dayfighter had proven itself to be fatally flawed. The aircraft was instead stripped of its weaponry and converted into a long-range reconnaissance platform instead. Designated the J1N1-C, which was changed to J1N1-R soon afterwards, the first 'Irvings' were encountered by the Allies over the Solomons. With the advent of night bombing raids on Japanese targets by USAAF heavy bombers, a number of J1N1-C/Rs were converted in the field into nightfighters through the fitment of oblique-firing 20 mm cannon. Designated the J1N1-C KAI, the makeshift interceptor proved successful enough for Nakajima to go into production with the dedicated J1N1-S Model 11 Gekko (Moonlight) nightfighter. The first of these entered service in August 1943, and the aircraft featuring a redesigned upper rear fuselage and obliquely-firing 20 mm cannon. Once in service, a number of Gekkos were fitted with radar, nose-mounted searchlights and additional 20 mm cannon in the nose.

138

Specification (all dimensions and performance data for J1N1-S)

Dimensions:
Length: 39 ft 11.5 in (12.18 m)
Wingspan: 55 ft 8.5 in (16.98 m)
Height: 14 ft 11.5 in (4.56 m)

Weights:
Empty: 10 670 lb (4840 kg)
Max T/O: 18 043 lb (8184 kg)

Performance:
Max Speed: 315 mph (507 kmh)
Range: 2330 miles (3750 km)
Powerplants: two Nakajima NK1F Sakae engines
Output: 2260 hp (1684 kW)

Armament:
two upward- and two downward-firing 20 mm cannon in fuselage

First Flight Date:
May 1941

Operator:
Japan

Production:
479

Allied codename: 'Irving'

Production of the nightfighter ended in December 1944, by which time J1N1-Ss had seen action in the Central and South-West Pacific, where it proved a worthy opponent for the B-24. However, the Gekko proved to be too slow to intercept B-29s over the home islands in 1945.

Right: Nakajima J1N1-S Gekko

Nakajima A6M2-N Zero Japan

Type: single-engined monoplane floatplane fighter   **Accommodation:** pilot

Development/History

Built in answer to an IJN requirement issued in September 1940 for a floatplane fighter capable of providing aerial support for an amphibious landing force, the A6M2-N was based closely on the Mitsubishi fighter of the same period. Designed for operation from the isolated lagoons and sheltered waterways that proliferated throughout the South-West and Central Pacific, the task of developing the Zero floatplane was given to Nakajima, as Mitsubishi was more than busy trying to produce sufficient carrier-based A6Ms to satisfy the IJN's burgeoning needs. The original order for the floatplane fighter was issued to Kawanishi and their advanced N1K1 Kyofu, but due to the immaturity of their programme, the IJN chose an interim Zero-based fighter to fulfil their immediate requirements. The work carried out by Nakajima to turn the A6M2 into the A6M2-N focused on the replacement of the undercarriage with a large central float and two outriggers, the addition of a small ventral fin so as to allow the pilot to maintain directional stability and the incorporation of an extra fuel tank within the float instead of beneath the now-occupied centre fuselage. The

first production aircraft entered IJN service in July 1942, and production was completed by September of the following year. Despite the central float restricting the A6M2-N's top speed to just 270 mph, the floatplane fighter retained much of the conventional Zero fighter's manoeuvrability, and it acquitted itself reasonably well over the Solomons and in the Aleutians.

Specification

Dimensions:
Length: 33 ft 1.5 in (10.10 m)
Wingspan: 39 ft 4.25 in (12.00 m)
Height: 14 ft 1.25 in (4.30 m)

Weights:
Empty: 4215 lb (1912 kg)
Max T/O: 6349 lb (2880 kg)

Performance:
Max Speed: 270 mph (435 kmh)
Range: 1108 miles (1784 km) with float tank
Powerplant: Nakajima NK1C Sakae 12
Output: 950 hp (708 kW)

Armament:
two 7.7 mm machine guns in nose, two 20 mm cannon in wings; provision for two underwing 132 lb (60 kg) bombs under wings

First Flight Date:
8 December 1941

Operator:
Japan

Production: 327

Allied codename: 'Rufe'

Right: Nakajima A6M2-N 'Rufe'

Nakajima Ki-84 Hayate Japan

Type: single-engined monoplane fighter   Accommodation: pilot

Development/History

The best JAAF fighter of the war, the Ki-84 Hayate (Gale) was built as a direct replacement for the venerable Ki-43. Combining a powerful radial engine with a well-built and properly amoured airframe, the 'Frank' suffered a prolonged gestation like most Japanese fighter designs due to engine unreliability and use of inferior quality materials. The primary powerplant maladies centred on the direct injection system of the Ha-45 engine, which proved to be labour intensive in respect to servicing between flights even once the fighter had reached the frontline. This in turn resulted in a high unserviceability rate amongst Ki-84-equipped sentais in the last year of the war, plus numerous operational accidents due to aircraft suffering engine failure in flight. No fewer than 125 service trials and pre-production aircraft were deemed necessary by the JAAF in order to resolve the engine problems, and this in turn delayed the fighter's operational debut until mid-1944. Ki-84s firstly engaged Allied forces over China, before being rushed to the Philippines following the American invasion in October 1944. When its engine was running as designed, the Ki-84 was

Specification (all dimensions and performance data for Ki-84-I-Ko)

Dimensions:
Length: 32 ft 6.5 in (9.92 m)
Wingspan: 36 ft 10.5 in (11.24 m)
Height: 11 ft 1 in (3.38 m)

Weights:
Empty: 5864 lb (2660 kg)
Max T/O: 8576 lb (3890 kg)

Performance:
Max Speed: 392 mph (631 kmh)
Range: 1025 miles (1650 km)
Powerplant: Nakajima Ha-45-21/-23/-25
Output: 1900-2000 hp (1417-1491 kW)

Armament:
two 12.7 mm machine guns in nose and two 20 mm cannon in wings

First Flight Date:
March 1943

Operator:
Japan

Production:
3514

Allied codename: 'Frank'

a fearsome opponent for any Allied fighter, and it more than held its own in the final aerial engagements of the war. Several sub-variants were produced during the Ki-84's brief production life, and these primarily differed in their weapons fits, although the -II models utilised a wooden rear fuselage in an effort to ease the strain on Japan's rapidly-diminishing supply of aluminium.

Right: Nakajima Ki-84-I-Ko Hayate

North American P-51A/Mustang I USA

Type: single-engined monoplane fighter　　**Accommodation:** pilot

Development/History

The Mustang has its origins in a British Purchasing Commission deal struck with North American in April 1940 for an advanced fighter to supplant the Spitfire. With the RAF facing an impending Luftwaffe onslaught, the agreement stipulated that the American company had to have a completed prototype – tailored to the British specifications – ready for flight within 120 days of the original submission. Fortunately, North American had already made a start independently of the British deal, their NA-73X design incorporating some of the lessons gleaned from aerial combat in Europe. Three days short of the required date the airframe was completed, and testing soon bore out the 'rightness' of the design, the aircraft (christened the 'Mustang I' by the British) handling beautifully thanks to its revolutionary semi-laminar flow airfoil wing. However, it was soon realised that the fighter's Allison V-1710 'ran out of steam' above 17,000 ft due to its lack of a supercharger. By that stage in the war, fighter combat was taking place at ceilings well in excess of 20,000 ft where the 'thin' air starved a conventionally aspirated engine, so the RAF Mustang Is were

fitted with cameras and relegated to the low-level tactical reconnaissance and army co-operation roles. The USAAF, too, realising that the Mustang was no good as a fighter above medium altitude, ordered a small number of A-36As and P-51As for ground attack tasks instead.

Specification

Dimensions:
Length: 32 ft 3 in (9.83 m)
Wingspan: 37 ft 0 in (11.28 m)
Height: 12 ft 2 in (3.71 m)

Weights:
Empty: 6550 lb (2971 kg)
Loaded Weight: 8800 lb (3992 kg)

Performance:
Max Speed: 387 mph (622 kmh)
Range: 1250 miles (2010 km) with external tanks
Powerplant: Allison V-1710-81
Output: 1200 hp (1014 kW)

Armament:
P-51A, four 0.50 in machine guns in wings

First Flight Date:
26 October 1940

Operators:
Canada, UK, USA

Production:
1228

Right: North American Mustang I AG633 of No II(AC) Sqn, RAF

North American P-51B/C/D/K Mustang USA

Type: single-engined monoplane fighter   **Accommodation:** pilot

Development/History

As detailed in the previous entry, the Mustang I's performance had let it down in the high-altitude dogfights that characterised air combat in Europe. However, the airframe itself was more than sound, so the RAF quickly searched for a replacement powerplant and came up with the Merlin 61. Once mated with this battle-proven engine, the aircraft's performance was startling – a communiqué of the findings was immediately sent to North American, and the rest is history. Car builder Packard was granted a licence to build the Merlin as the Packard V-1650, and North American followed the British lead in mating surplus P-51A airframes with the 'new' powerplant. The Merlin-powered P-51B made its combat debut over Europe in December 1943, just when the USAAF's much-vaunted daylight bomber campaign had begun to falter due to unsustainable losses. Here was their 'knight in shinning armour', capable of escorting B-17s and B-24s throughout their hazardous missions. Over the next 19 months of war in Europe, the Mustang steadily became the dominant USAAF fighter. The RAF, too, got their hands on well over 1000 Merlin-powered

aircraft through Lend-Lease arrangements. In total over 14,819 P-51s were built by North American, plus a further 200 under-licence in Australia. The fighter continued to serve in a frontline capacity with the USAF into the early 1950s, and further afield in Central and South America until the 1970s.

Specification (all dimensions and performance data for P-51D)

Dimensions:
Length: 32 ft 3 in (9.83 m)
Wingspan: 37 ft 0 in (11.28 m)
Height: 12 ft 2 in (3.71 m)

Weights:
Empty: 7635 lb (3463 kg)
Max T/O: 12 100 lb (5488 kg)

Performance:
Max Speed: 437 mph (703 kmh)
Range: 1650 miles (2655 km) with external tanks
Powerplant: Packard V-1650-7
Output: 1720 hp (1283 kW)

Armament:
six 0.50 in machine guns in wings; up to 2000 lb (907 kg) bombs or six 5 in (12.7 cm) rocket projectiles under wings

First Flight Date:
13 October 1942

Operators:
Australia, China, the Netherlands, New Zealand, South Africa, UK, USA

Production:
9493

Right: Royal Australian Air Force North American P-51K Mustang A68-585 of No 84 Sqn, Far East Air Force

Northrop P-61 Black Widow USA

Type: twin-engined monoplane fighter   **Accommodation:** three-man crew

Development/History

The first aircraft to be purposely designed as a radar-equipped nightfighter, Northrop's P-61 Black Widow was heavily influenced by early RAF combat experience with radar-equipped aircraft in 1940/41. Built to fulfil a late 1940 US Army Air Corps requirement, the proposed fighter was essentially designed around the bulky Radiation Laboratory SCR-720 radar, which was mounted in the aircraft's nose. The company's design was accepted the following year, and Northrop immediately went to work building two XP-61 prototypes and 13 YP-61 evaluation aircraft. The Black Widow proved to be the largest fighter ever procured for frontline service by the USAAF, its substantial airframe being capable of housing a dorsal barbette of four 0.50-in Browning machine guns and four ventrally-mounted 20 mm cannon. After initial structural and radar problems, the aircraft was finally issued to a frontline unit (the 481st Night Fighter Group) in March 1944, and both ETO and Pacific squadrons went into action almost simultaneously that spring – the honour of scoring the first kill (a Japanese 'Betty' bomber) went to the 6th Night Fighter Squadron on 6

148

July 1944. Some 706 Black Widows were built in three distinct variants by Northrop, and the type saw action as a night intruder operating against ground targets as well as in its designated role.

Specification (all dimensions and performance data for P-61B)

Dimensions:
Length: 49 ft 7 in (15.11 m)
Wingspan: 66 ft 0 in (20.11 m)
Height: 14 ft 8 in (4.47 m)

Weights:
Empty: 22 000 lb (9979 kg)
Max T/O: 38 000 lb (17 237 kg)

Performance:
Max Speed: 366 mph (589 kmh)
Range: 3000 miles (4828 km) with external tanks
Powerplants: two Pratt & Whitney R-2800-65 Double Wasp engines
Output: 4000 hp (2982 kW)

Armament:
four ventral 0.50 in machine guns and four 20 mm cannon in remote-controlled dorsal turret; provision for 6400 lb (2903 kg) of underwing ordnance

First Flight Date:
26 May 1942

Operators:
USA

Production:
706

Right: Northrop
P-61B-15 Black Widow
42-39728

Polikarpov I-16 USSR

Type: single-engined monoplane fighter   **Accommodation:** pilot

Development/History

The world's first cantilever low wing monoplane and retractable undercarriage fighter to enter frontline service, the I-16 was an incredibly advanced design for its time, but by the outbreak of World War 2, it had been well and truly left behind by more modern fighter types. Despite this fact, the I-16 still equipped two-thirds of all Soviet air force fighter units at the time of the German invasion in June 1941. Indeed, as a sign of just how revered the I-16 was in the USSR, although production had been stopped in 1940, Polikarpov was ordered to re-open the line just 12 months later! The first I-16s had entered service in the Soviet Union in early 1935, the fighter being powered by a reverse-engineered Wright Cyclone (designated the Shvetsov M-25). Throughout its long production life, the fighter was periodically upgraded through the fitment of uprated Shvetsov engines and improved armament. The I-16 first saw action with the Republican forces in the Spanish Civil War, some 278 being supplied by the USSR. It was also the primary Soviet fighter during the Nomonhan Incident with Japan in 1939, where it suffered terrible losses at the hands of the

Ki-27 and A5M. Later that same year the I-16 bore the brunt of the fighting with Finland in the Winter War of 1939-40, before being thrown into the fray against the Luftwaffe in June 1941. The I-16 was finally retired from frontline service in 1943.

Specification (all dimensions and performance data for I-16 *Tip 10*)

Dimensions:
Length: 19 ft 11.15 in (6.07 m)
Wingspan: 29 ft 6.33 in (9.00 m)
Height: 8 ft 4.75 in (2.56 m)

Weights:
Empty: 2976 lb (1350 kg)
Normal Loaded: 3781 lb (1715 kg)

Performance:
Max Speed: 273 mph (440 kmh)
Range: 497 miles (800 km)
Powerplant: Shvetsov M-25A
Output: 750 hp (578 kW)

Armament:
two 7.62 mm machine guns in nose and two in wings; provision for two-six underwing 82 mm rockets or up to 441 lb (200 kg) bombs under wings

First Flight Date:
31 December 1933

Operators:
China, Finland, Spain, USSR

Production:
8644 (all models, including I-16UTI two-seat trainer)

Right: Polikarpov I-16 Tip 6

Polikarpov I-152 (I-15bis) USSR

Type: single-engined biplane fighter   Accommodation: pilot

Development/History

Although Polikarpov earned the distinction of building the world's first 'modern' monoplane interceptor in the I-16, it was also a major manufacturer of biplane fighters as well. Indeed, the revolutionary I-15 biplane had flown just months prior to the I-16, its distinctive 'gulled' upper wing and I-type interplane struts giving the barrel-shaped fighter a distinctive appearance. Blessed with incredible manoeuvrability, a respectable top speed and potent armament, the I-15 proved popular both in the USSR and in Spain, where it saw much action in the Spanish Civil War. As a direct result of feedback from the latter conflict, Polikarpov redesigned the I-15 without the 'gulled' upper wing centre section, which pilots criticised for restricting their view of the ground in front of them on take-off and landing. Other improvements included the adoption of a long chord cowling for the Shvetsov M-25 radial and increased fuel capacity. The I-15 was duly replaced on the production line by the I-15bis (later redesignated the I-152) in late 1937. The fighter was subsequently used in the same conflicts as the I-16, often flying alongside the

monoplane Polikarpov. Although production ended in early 1939, substantial numbers of I-152s remained in service with the Soviet air force well into 1942.

Specification

Dimensions:
Length: 20 ft 7 in (6.27 m)
Wingspan: 33 ft 5.5 in (10.20 m)
Height: 9 ft 2.25 in (2.80 m)

Weights:
Empty: 2888 lb (1310 kg)
Max T/O: 4044 lb (1834 kg)

Performance:
Max Speed: 226 mph (364 kmh)
Range: 280 miles (450 km)
Powerplant: Shvetsov M-25V
Output: 775 hp (578 kW)

Armament:
two 7.62 mm machine guns in nose and two in wings

First Flight Date:
early 1937

Operators:
China, Finland, Spain, USSR

Production:
2408

Right: Polikarpov I-152 (I-15bis)

Polikarpov I-153 (I-15ter) USSR

Type: single-engined biplane fighter **Accommodation:** pilot

Development/History

The final word in the Polikarpov family of biplane fighters, the I-153 boasted a considerably more powerful Shvetsov radial and a retractable undercarriage, as well as the 'gull' wing centre section. Despite other manufacturers the world over embracing the monoplane fighter that he had pioneered in the early 1930s, Nikolai Polikarpov refused to abandon the biplane fighter, and the first I-153s entered frontline service as late as May 1939. No production variants of the basic I-153 were introduced during the fighter's brief production life, although there were occasional armament modifications carried out 'in the field' by the Soviet air force themselves. Polikarpov delivered its last I-153 in late 1940, and although in production for barely 18 months, no fewer than 3437 had been built in that time. Examples were supplied to China in 1940, who used them against the Japanese in a repeat of the Nomonhan Incident of the year before. Finland also made use of 11 captured examples following the 1939-40 Winter War, this number being doubled with the acquisition of a further 11 from captured stocks held by the Germans. Heavily involved in the opening months of the war on the Eastern Front, I-153s remained an important part of the Soviet fighter force into 1942, when they were relegated to the no less hazardous ground attack role.

Specification

Dimensions:
Length: 20 ft 3 in (6.17 m)
Wingspan: 32 ft 9.75 in (10.00 m)
Height: 9 ft 2.25 in (2.80 m)

Weights:
Empty: 3200 lb (1452 kg)
Max T/O: 4652 lb (2110 kg)

Performance:
Max Speed: 280 mph (450 kmh)
Range: 292 miles (470 km)
Powerplant: Shvetsov M-62R
Output: 1000 hp (746 kW)

Armament:
four 7.62 mm or 12.7 mm machine guns in nose; max bombload of 441 lb (200 kg) or six 82 mm rocket projectiles under wings

First Flight Date:
mid-1938

Operators:
China, Finland, USSR

Production:
3437

Right: Captured Polikarpov I-153 of the Finnish air force

P.Z.L. P.11 Poland

Type: single-engined high-wing fighter   **Accommodation:** pilot

Development/History

The final incarnation of the successful P.Z.L. family of high-wing fighters that could trace its lineage back to the two-seat P.W.S.1 of 1927, the P.11 was the staple fighter of the Polish Air Force at the time of the German invasion on 1 September 1939. Effectively an upgraded P.7, stressed to accept the more powerful Bristol Mercury engine in place of the Jupiter VII.F from the same source, the P.11 entered service in late 1933. Capable of reasonable speeds, highly manoeuvrable and well armed, the P.Z.L. fighter was also licence-built in Romania by I.A.R., where it was re-engined with the Gnome-Rhône Mistral/Jupiter engine. After a period of several years out of production, P.Z.L. was ordered to re-open the line as it became obvious that war with Germany was inevitable. The new P.11g was to be powered by the 840 hp (626 kW) Mercury VIII engine, but it had only flown in prototype form by the time of the invasion. Despite being truly outclassed by their opponents in Bf 109s and Bf 110s, the 12 squadrons of P.11s that opposed the German aerial assault on Poland claimed 125 Luftwaffe aircraft destroyed for the loss of 114 of their own number during the first few days of the invasion.

Specification (all dimensions and performance data for P.11c)

Dimensions:
Length: 24 ft 9.25 in (7.55 m)
Wingspan: 35 ft 2 in (10.72 m)
Height: 9 ft 4.25 in (2.85 m)

Weights:
Empty: 2529 lb (1147 kg)
Normal Loaded: 3968 lb (1800 kg)

Performance:
Max Speed: 242 mph (389 kmh)
Range: 435 miles (700 km)
Powerplant: P.Z.L. Mercury VS2/VIS2
Output: 600-645 hp (447-481 kW)

Armament:
two 7.7 mm machine guns in forward fuselage and two in wings; max load of 110 lb (50 kg) bomb under each wing

First Flight Date:
August 1931

Operators:
Poland, Romania

Production:
258 by P.Z.L. and approximately 80 by I.A.R. of Romania

Right: P.Z.L. P.11c of 112 Eskadron

P.Z.L. P.24 Poland

Type: single-engined high-wing fighter   **Accommodation:** pilot

Development/History

A refined P.11c produced by P.Z.L. for export, the P.24 was designed to accept the most powerful radial engines then in production. Aside from boasting more horsepower than its predecessor, the P.24 was also fitted with better armament in the form of a pair of 20 mm cannon and two 7.92 mm machine guns. The first country to order the P.24 was Turkey, who bought 40 in flyaway condition and a further 20 in kit form. These aircraft were a mix of A- and C-models, the latter being similar in specification to the all machine-gun armed P.24B, but with more aerodynamic refinements. The availability of the uprated Gnome-Rhône 14N 07 resulted in the production of the P.24F/G (ex-A- and B-models, respectively), and a number of the Turkish aircraft were suitably re-engined. A Greek order for 36 P.36s was fitted out with the new engine prior to delivery, whilst Romanian aircraft built under-licence by I.A.R. used the indigenous I.A.R.-K 14-II C32 in place of the Gnome-Rhône. The delivery of the last Romanian aircraft (44 built, essentially to P-24A specification) in the late autumn of 1939 signalled the end of P.24 production, and

Specification (all dimensions and performance data for P.24F)

Dimensions:
Length: 24 ft 11.5 in (7.60 m)
Wingspan: 35 ft 0.75 in (10.68 m)
Height: 8 ft 10.25 in (2.69 m)

Weights:
Empty: 2936 lb (1332 kg)
Max T/O: 4409 lb (2000 kg)

Performance:
Max Speed: 267 mph (430 kmh)
Range: 342 miles (550 km)
Powerplant: Gnome-Rhône 14N 07
Output: 970 hp (718 kW)

Armament:
two 7.92 mm machine guns in forward fuselage and two 20 mm cannon in wings

First Flight Date:
May 1933

Operators:
Bulgaria, Greece, Romania, Turkey

Production:
168

surviving examples in Greece, Romania and Bulgaria saw wartime action either for or against the Axis powers through to early 1942.

Right: P.Z.L. P.24F of the Turkish air force

Reggianne Re.2000/2001/2002 Italy

Type: single-engined monoplane fighter

Accommodation: pilot

Development/History

A subsidiary of large Italian aviation concern Caproni, Reggiane produced a family of fighters modelled closely on the American Seversky P-35 of the late 1930s. The first to fly was the Re.2000, which also subsequently enjoyed the most success in terms of volume production. Designed by Roberto G Longhi, the aircraft had an all-metal airframe and five-spar wing embodying integral fuel tanks. Powered by a Piaggio P.XI radial, the Re.2000 was ordered in modest quantities by the *Regia Aeronautica*, who already had the comparable Fiat G.50 and Macchi C.200 in service, or on order. Although just 17 aircraft were supplied to the air force, and a further eight to the *Aviazione Ausiliaria per la Regia Marina*, the Re.2000 was ordered in good numbers by Sweden (60) and Hungary (70). Indeed, the latter operator also acquired licence-production rights, and built a further 203 as the Mavag Héjja II, powered by the Gnome-Rhône 14Kfs radial. In July 1940 Reggiane commenced testing an Alfa Romeo RA.1000 (licence-built Daimler-Benz DB 601) equipped Re.2000, which was redesignated the Re.2001. Some 252 were eventually built for *Regia*

Specification (all dimensions and performance data for Re.2000)

Dimensions:
Length: 26 ft 2.5 in (7.99 m)
Wingspan: 36 ft 1 in (11.00 m)
Height: 10 ft 6 in (3.20 m)

Weights:
Empty: 4563 lb (2070 kg)
Loaded Weight: 6349 lb (2880 kg)

Performance:
Max Speed: 329 mph (529 kmh)
Range: 870 miles (1400 km)
Powerplant: Piaggio P.XI RC 40
Output: 1040 hp (775 kW)

Armament:
two 12.7 mm machine guns in nose

First Flight Date:
24 May 1939

Operators:
Germany, Hungary, Italy, Sweden

Production:
835

Aeronautica, and these entered service in mid-1942. However, a shortage of engines soon saw the RA.1000 replaced by the Piaggio P.XIX, resulting in the creation of the Re.2002. Of the resulting 224 aircraft that were constructed, most were delivered to the Luftwaffe after the September 1943 armistice, and they put them to effective use as ground attack aircraft primarily over occupied France.

Right: Reggiane Re.2000

Reggianne Re.2005 Italy

Type: single-engined monoplane fighter   Accommodation: pilot

Development/History

Like the final generation Fiat G.55 and Macchi
C.205V, the Re.2005 came along just too late
to make any real impression on the Allied
invasion of Italy. Of the three fighters, the
Reggiane design was the one produced in the
smallest numbers, yet is possessed the best
performance figures of the trio. Powered by the
familiar Fiat-built DB 605A engine, the Re.2005
was capable of attaining speeds of 421 mph
thanks to its light weight and drag free
airframe. Development of the aircraft was
undertaken by Roberto Longhi in late 1941,
and the first prototype took to the skies as
early as May 1942. However, the decision to
acquire the Re.2005 was delayed until February
of the following year, when a large order was
placed for 34 pre-series Re.2005s and 750
production standard fighters. Due to this
hiatus, only the pre-series aircraft had been
built when Italy surrendered, some 20 of these
managing to see brief operational service with
the *Regia Aeronautica* on Sicily prior to the
armistice. A further 11 Re.2005s were
subsequently requisitioned from Reggiane by
the Luftwaffe.

Specification

Dimensions:

Length: 28 ft 7.75 in (7.99 m)
Wingspan: 36 ft 1 in (11.00 m)
Height: 10 ft 4 in (3.15 m)

Weights:

Empty: 5732 lb (2600 kg)
Loaded Weight: 7959 lb (3610 kg)

Performance:

Max Speed: 421 mph (678 kmh)
Range: 776 miles (1250 km)
Powerplant: Fiat RA.1050 RC58 Tifone (licence-built Daimler-Benz DB 605A)
Output: 1475 hp (1100 kW)

Armament:

three 20 mm cannon in nose and propeller hub
and two 12.7 mm machine guns wings

First Flight Date:

10 May 1942

Operator:

Italy

Production:

37

*Right: The second
prototype Reggiane
Re.2005*

Republic P-47 Thunderbolt USA

Type: single-engined monoplane fighter   **Accommodation:** pilot

Development/History

The original P-47 design was produced to meet a 1940 USAAC requirement for a lightweight interceptor similar in size and stature to the Spitfire and Bf 109. Powered by Allison's ubiquitous V-1710-39 1150 hp inline engine, the XP-47A was to boast just two 0.50-in machine guns as armament and lacked any protective armour or self-sealing tanks. However, combat reports filtering in from Europe proved the folly of a lightweight fighter, and the USAAC modified its design requirements to include an eight-gun fitment, heavy armour plating and a self-sealing fuel system. Republic responded with an all-new design, powered, crucially, by a turbocharged R-2800 Double Wasp radial engine. Despite initial reliability problems with its powerplant, production of the Republic design forged ahead. The first P-47Bs joined the Eighth Air Force in Britain in late 1942 to undertake the much needed escort role for the latter's growing heavy bomber force. Built to absorb much damage, and rock steady as a gun platform, the Thunderbolt was soon holding its own not only against the Luftwaffe, but also the JAAF and IJN in the Pacific and CBI. The arrival of the definitive P-47D in late 1943 was followed by the advent of the 'bubble top' Thunderbolt, which duly became the favoured mount over the 'razorback' 'Jug'. Some 15,677 Thunderbolts were eventually built, and a number of P-47Ns soldiered on with the Air National Guard, and a handful of other air arms, into the early 1950s.

Specification (all dimensions and performance data for P-47N)

Dimensions:
Length: 36 ft 1 in (11.00 m)
Wingspan: 42 ft 7 in (12.98 m)
Height: 14 ft 8 in (4.47 m)

Weights:
Empty: 11 170 lb (5067 kg)
Max T/O: 20 700 lb (9390 kg)

Performance:
Max Speed: 467 mph (751 kmh)
Range: 2350 miles (3782 km) with external tanks
Powerplant: Pratt & Whitney R-2800-57C/-77 Double Wasp
Output: 2800 hp (2088 kW)

Armament:
eight 0.50 in machine guns wings in wings; two 1000 lb (454 kg) or three 500 lb (227 kg) bombs or ten 5 in (12.7 mm) rockets externally

First Flight Date:
6 May 1941 (XP-47B) and September 1944 (XP-47N)

Operators:
Brazil, France, Mexico, UK, USA, USSR

Production:
15 683 (1816 P-47Ns)

Right: Republic P-47N-5 Thunderbolt 44-88335

Supermarine Spitfire Mk I/II UK

Type: single-engined monoplane fighter

Accommodation: pilot

Development/History

The only British fighter to remain in production throughout World War 2, the exploits of the Supermarine Spitfire are legendary. Over 20,000 were produced in mark numbers ranging from I through to 24, this total also including over 1000 built as dedicated Seafire fleet fighters for the Royal Navy. Designed by Reginald J Mitchell following his experiences with the RAF's Schneider Trophy winning Supermarine floatplanes of the 1920s and 30s, prototype Spitfire K5054 first took to the skies on 6 March 1936, powered by the soon to be equally famous Rolls-Royce Merlin I engine. However, due to production problems encountered with the revolutionary stressed-skin construction of the fighter, it was to be another two-and-a-half years before the first examples entered service with Fighter Command. Spitfire Mk Is and IIs served only briefly in frontline squadrons with the RAF (exclusively on the Channel Front) once the war had started, but their pilots were responsible for achieving impressive scores against the all-conquering Luftwaffe during the Battles of France and Britain. Although early-mark Spitfires were notorious for their light armament, overheating engines due to inadequate cooling and short range, many of the pilots that flew the Mk I and IIs regarded the first production machines as the best handling of the breed, being a 'true aviator's aircraft' due to its excellent power to weight ratio and beautifully harmonised flying controls.

Specification (all dimensions and performance data for Spitfire Mk IA)

Dimensions:
Length: 29 ft 11 in (9.12 m)
Wingspan: 36 ft 10 in (11.23 m)
Height: 11 ft 5 in (3.48 m)

Weights:
Empty: 4810 lb (2182 kg)
Loaded Weight: 5844 lb (2651 kg)

Performance:
Max Speed: 355 mph (571 kmh)
Range: 575 miles (925 km)
Powerplant: Rolls-Royce Merlin II/III
Output: 1030 hp (768 kW)

Armament:
eight 0.303 in machine guns wings

First Flight Date:
5 March 1936

Operators:
Australia, Canada, New Zealand, UK

Production:
1567 Mk Is and 921 Mk IIs

Right: Supermarine Spitfire Mk IB R6923 of No 92 Sqn

Supermarine Spitfire Mk V/VI UK

Type: single-engined monoplane fighter   Accommodation: pilot

Development/History

As the first Spitfire variant to see extensive service outside of Britain, the Mk V fought the Axis alliance over North Africa, the Mediterranean and in Australasia. The first attempts by Supermarine to upgrade the Mk I/II had seen the Mk III produced, the latter fighter boasting a 1480 hp Merlin XX, revised airframe, stronger undercarriage, clipped wings and a retractable tailwheel. However, all these improvements combined to slow down the production rate of the desperately needed fighter, so an order for 1000 was cancelled, and the much simpler Mk V was chosen instead. Getting the improved aircraft into the frontline was a matter of great importance, as the arrival of new German fighters (the Bf 109F and the Fw 190A) on the Channel front had rendered the early marks ineffective. In order to speed up the delivery process, the Mk V had been created by simply pairing a Mk I or II fuselage with the new Merlin 45 engine, and the new combination proved to be so successful that some 6479 airframes would eventually be built. Thanks to this overwhelming production run, the Mk V bore the brunt of Fighter Command operations on

virtually all fronts to which the RAF was committed between 1941 and late 1943. A specialist variant derived from the Mk V was the high-altitude optimised Mk VI, which used a 'tweaked' Merlin 47, a four-bladed propeller and had a pressurised cockpit.

Specification (all dimensions and performance data for Spitfire Mk VC)

Dimensions:
Length: 29 ft 11 in (9.12 m)
Wingspan: 36 ft 10 in (11.23 m)
Height: 11 ft 5 in (3.48 m)

Weights:
Empty: 5100 lb (2313 kg)
Loaded Weight: 6785 lb (3078 kg)

Performance:
Max Speed: 374 mph (602 kmh)
Range: 470 miles (756 km)
Powerplant: Rolls-Royce Merlin 45/50/55/56
Output: 1470 hp (1096 kW)

Armament:
eight 0.303 in machine guns or four 20 mm cannon in wings; provision for one 500 lb (227 kg) or two 250 lb (113 kg) bombs externally

First Flight Date:
December 1940

Operators:
Australia, Canada, Egypt, France, Greece, Italy, New Zealand, Portugal, South Africa, Turkey, UK, USA, USSR

Production:
6472 Mk Vs and 100 Mk VIs

Right: Supermarine Spitfire Mk VB trop EP689 of No 145 Sqn

Supermarine Spitfire Mk VII/VIII UK

Type: single-engined monoplane fighter

Accommodation: pilot

Development/History

Despite having mark numbers earlier than the Mk IX, both the Mks VII and VIII actually entered service well after it due to the substantial redesign embodied in both variants. Utilising the Merlin 60 series engine, with its two-stage, two-speed supercharger, six port exhaust, four-bladed propeller, longer nose and symmetrical underwing radiators, the Mk VII/VIII combined these powerplant improvements with a reworked, strengthened fuselage and revised 'C' wing that was fitted with shorter span ailerons and additional fuel tankage. Finally, most aircraft also had a distinctive pointed fin and rudder. The Mk VII was built as a specialist high altitude interceptor, with extended wing tips and a pressurised cabin, whilst the Mk VIII was built to an identical specification, but lacked both the former features, as it was intended to be a conventional fighter-bomber. The Mk VII started to enter squadron service in September 1942, and the fighter scored its first kill later that same month at 38,000 ft (11,580 m). The Mk VIII made its service debut in 1943, and went on to equip units in the Mediterranean, the Balkans, the Middle and Far East and Burma. Aside from the RAF, the Royal Australian Air Force was the major user of the Mk VIII, receiving no less than 410 examples from October 1943.

Specification (all dimensions and performance data for Spitfire LF VIII)

Dimensions:

Length: 31 ft 3.5 in (9.54 m)
Wingspan: 36 ft 10 in (11.23 m)
Height: 12 ft 7.75 in (3.86 m)

Weights:

Empty: 5800 lb (2631 kg)
Loaded Weight: 7767 lb (3523 kg)

Performance:

Max Speed: 404 mph (650 kmh)
Range: 1180 miles (1900 km) with external tanks
Powerplant: Rolls-Royce Merlin 66
Output: 1720 hp (1282 kW)

Armament:

two 20 mm cannon and four 0.303 in machine guns in wings; provision for 1000 lb (454 kg) bombload externally

First Flight Date:

April 1942 (Mk VII)

Operators:

Australia, UK

Production:

140 Mk VIIs and 1658 Mk VIIIs

Right: Supermarine Spitfire Mk LF VIIIs A58-315/-395/-405 and -409 of the RAAF

Supermarine Spitfire Mk IX UK

Type: single-engined monoplane fighter   **Accommodation:** pilot

Development/History

Through the desperate years of 1941-42, the Spitfire was outclassed by firstly the Bf 109F/G and then the potent Fw 190. Indeed, it was the appearance of the 'Butcher bird' from Focke-Wulf on the Channel front in September 1941 which provided the impetus for a new version of Spitfire to help restore the balance – thus was born the Spitfire Mk IX. Built as a stop-gap fighter until the comprehensively re-engineered Mks VII and VIII could be put into production, the IX comprised a lightly-modified Mk V airframe fitted with an uprated Merlin 61 engine. Despite its temporary nature, the 'new' fighter was so warmly received by frontline units within Fighter Command that no less than 5665 were built between 1942-45. The secret to the 'new' Spitfire's success can be directly attributed to its Rolls-Royce powerplant, which had been fitted with a two-stage/two-speed supercharger that would cut in automatically at pre-determined altitudes, but could also be manually controlled at lower ceilings. The earlier Mk V, powered by the Merlin 45, had had to make do with a single-stage/single-speed supercharger, which was fine at low to medium altitude, but rather

Specification (all dimensions and performance data for Spitfire F IX)

Dimensions:

Length: 31 ft 1 in (9.47 m)
Wingspan: 36 ft 10 in (11.23 m)
Height: 12 ft 7.75 in (3.86 m)

Weights:

Empty: 5800-6200 lb (2631-2812 kg)
Max T/O: 9500 lb (4309 kg)

Performance:

Max Speed: 408 mph (657 kmh)
Range: 980 miles (1577 km) with external tanks
Powerplant: Rolls-Royce Merlin 61
Output: 1565 hp (1167 kW)

Armament:

F IXB, two 20 mm cannon and four 0.303 in machine guns in wings; provision for 1000 lb (454 kg) bombload externally

First Flight Date:

early 1942

Operators:

Australia, Canada, New Zealand, South Africa, UK, USA, USSR

Production:

5665

'breathless' at the more rarefied ceilings above 20,000 ft – the chosen battleground of the Jagdwaffe. The Merlin 61 changed all this, however, as its more powerful supercharger forced a greater volume of air through the engine cylinders, and thus prevented performance tailing off in the thinner altitudes that Fighter Command was having to fight in.

Right: Supermarine Spitfire LF IX MK177

Supermarine Spitfire Mk XII UK

Type: single-engined monoplane fighter

Accommodation: pilot

Development/History

This interim model Spitfire was the first to use the newly-developed Rolls-Royce Griffon powerplant, which had been designed with one-third greater capacity to allow improved levels of horsepower to be achieved. The airframe initially developed to harness this power was the Mk IV (later redesignated the Mk XX), but a role change for the fighter mid-development saw the once high-altitude optimised Griffon Spitfire altered to achieve its best performance at low level in order to counter Fw 190 'hit and run' raiders that were causing problems along the south coast of England. The resulting Mk XII featured a restyled engine cowling to house the larger Griffon, clipped 'C' wings for optimum performance 'down low' and a pointed rudder. With the airframe employed based closely on the Mk V, and then the Mk VIII, the Mk XII had no extra fuel capacity, and with the Griffon being appreciably 'thirstier' than its predecessor, the fighter's range was even worse than the previously short-legged Merlin Spitfire. However, the role for which the Mk XII was used did not require long searching patrols to be flown, and the first of just 100 was delivered to the RAF for two home defence squadrons in February 1943. The Mk XII proved successful in its chosen role, and was also used for shipping reconnaissance and fighter sweeps over France until finally replaced by the vastly improved Mk XIV in September 1944.

Specification

Dimensions:
Length: 31 ft 10 in (9.70 m)
Wingspan: 32 ft 7 in (9.93 m)
Height: 11 ft 0 in (3.35 m)

Weights:
Empty: 5600 lb (2540 kg)
Loaded Weight: 7400 lb (3357 kg)

Performance:
Max Speed: 393 mph (632 kmh)
Range: 493 miles (793 km) with external tanks
Powerplant: Rolls-Royce Griffon III/IV
Output: 1735 hp (1294 kW)

Armament:
two 20 mm cannon and four 0.303 in machine guns in wings; provision for one 500 lb (227 kg) or two 250 lb (113 kg) bombs externally

First Flight Date:
24 August 1942

Operator:
UK

Production:
100

*Right: Supermarine
Spitfire Mk XII MB882*

Supermarine Spitfire Mk XIV UK

Type: single-engined monoplane fighter

Accommodation: pilot

Development/History

The Mk XIV was without a doubt the Spitfire that commanded the most respect! The reason for this was simple – the 'state-of-the-art' Griffon 65/66 engine produced almost too much torque for the essentially pre-war design to handle, particularly when gathering speed for take-off. Indeed, a number of early Mk XIV pilots reported that the aircraft felt as if it wanted to 'rotate around the propeller', rather than the other way round! These longitudinal problems aside, the Spitfire Mk XIV was an awesome fighter to fly thanks to the generous levels of horsepower cranked out by its Griffon engine – 2050 hp to be precise. Granted, it may have 'put a bit of weight on round the middle', thanks to Supermarine engineers strengthening the fuselage in preparation for the fitment of the new powerplant, but the standard production F XIVE could nevertheless attain a top speed of almost 450 mph, and climb to 43,000 ft. Only 957 production Mk XIVs were built, with perhaps the type's finest hour coming in mid-1944 when its straight-line speed was used to great effect to counter the V1 menace during Air Defence Great Britain patrols over south-east England – the Spitfire

XIV could outpace all other frontline types, including the Tempest V. A considerable number of Griffon Spitfires were also sent to units in the Far East in the last year of the war, although in the most part they arrived too late to see action against the Japanese.

Specification

Dimensions:
Length: 31 ft 8 in (9.96 m)
Wingspan: 36 ft 10 in (11.23 m)
Height: 12 ft 8 in (3.86 m)

Weights:
Empty: 6600 lb (2994 kg)
Max T/O: 9772 lb (4433 kg)

Performance:
Max Speed: 448 mph (721 kmh)
Range: 850 miles (1368 km) with external tanks
Powerplant: Rolls-Royce Griffon 65
Output: 2050 hp (1528 kW)

Armament:
two 20 mm cannon and four 0.303 in machine guns in wings; provision for one 500 lb (227 kg) or two 250 lb (113 kg) bombs externally

First Flight Date:
early 1943

Operator:
Australia, Canada, New Zealand, UK

Production:
957

Right: Supermarine Spitfire F XIV of No 610 Sqn

Supermarine Spitfire Mk XVI UK

Type: single-engined monoplane fighter

Accommodation: pilot

Development/History

Unlike the numerous Spitfire variants that preceded the Mk XVI, this version of the famous Vickers-Supermarine design was used principally as a ground-attack aircraft, rather than in its more familiar fighter role. This change in function, if not in form, graphically illustrated that the true versatility of the design had been realised during its long production life. Initially externally similar in appearance to its more common precursor the Mk IX, the Mk XVI was deemed to warrant a new mark number because it was powered by a fully-imported, US-built, Packard-Merlin 266 engine. The first Mk XVIs were issued to frontline units in the autumn of 1944, these machines having the traditional high-back fuselage and pointed rudder of the late-build Mk IXs. However, in response to requests from pilots for better visibility (aircrew had complained about the obstructed view back over their shoulders since the first Mk Is entered service in summer of 1938!), a cut-down fuselage version that boasted a bubble canopy was introduced from February 1945. Thanks to the exceptional power output of the Packard-Merlin 266 at low-level, the Mk XVI

Specification (all dimensions and performance data for Spitfire F XVIE)

Dimensions:
Length: 31 ft 1 in (9.47 m)
Wingspan: 36 ft 10 in (11.23 m)
Height: 12 ft 7.75 in (3.86 m)

Weights:
Empty: 5800-6200 lb (2631-2812 kg)
Max T/O: 9500 lb (4309 kg)

Performance:
Max Speed: 408 mph (657 kmh)
Range: 980 miles (1577 km) with external tanks
Powerplant: Rolls-Royce Merlin 66/ Packard Merlin 266
Output: 1720 hp (1282 kW)

Armament:
two 20 mm cannon and two 0.50 in machine guns in wings; provision for 1000 lb (454 kg) bombload externally

First Flight Date:
mid-1944

Operators:
Australia, Canada, New Zealand, South Africa, UK

Production:
1054

became the ideal candidate for close attack work in support of the Allied armies fighting their way into Germany. So successful was the aircraft at precision bombing that in the last year of the war, the Spitfire Mk XVI proved to be more usefully employed by the Allies as a dedicated ground attack aircraft than in its proven day fighter role.

Right: Supermarine Spitfire F XIVE of the RAF's Central Gunnery School

Supermarine Seafire Mk I/II/III UK

Type: single-engined monoplane fighter   **Accommodation:** pilot

Development/History

Delayed from reaching production by the RAF's priority on all Spitfire production, the first navalised example did not fly until January 1942 – almost two years after the Navy had inquired whether a 'Sea Spitfire' could be produced. Although not ideally suited to carrier deck operations due to its narrow-track undercarriage and less than robust construction, the Seafire nevertheless provided the Fleet Air Arm with its first truly modern fighter of the conflict. No less than 20 frontline units received Seafires during World War 2, and the aircraft saw action over North Africa, Norway, Sicily, the Normandy beaches, Western Europe and the Far East. The first aircraft provided to the fleet were ex-RAF Mk VBs, fitted with a vee frame arrestor hook, a strengthened undercarriage and catapult spool. Some 166 Mk VBs were converted into Seafire Mk IBs and delivered between February 1942 and July 1943. The next variant to enter service was the Mk II, which was based on the Mk VC, and retained the latter's non-folding wings. Three sub-variants were built, using different versions of the Merlin engine or incorporating cameras. The final (and most numerous)

Specification (all dimensions and performance data for Seafire F III)

Dimensions:
Length: 30 ft 2.5 in (9.21 m)
Wingspan: 36 ft 10 in (11.23 m)
Height: 11 ft 5.5 in (3.49 m)

Weights:
Empty: 6204 lb (2814 kg)
Loaded Weight: 7640 lb (3465 kg)

Performance:
Max Speed: 348 mph (560 kmh)
Range: 725 miles (1167 km) with external tank
Powerplant: Rolls-Royce Merlin 55
Output: 1470 hp (1096 kW)

Armament:
two 20 mm cannon and four 0.303 in machine guns in wings; provision for one 500 lb (227 kg) or two 250 lb (113 kg) bombs externally

First Flight Date:
7 January 1942

Operator:
UK

Production:
2408 (all models)

wartime Seafire variant was the Mk III, which was fully navalised in that it at last had folding wings in order to maximise deck storage space – it was also powered by a latter generation Merlin 55, turning a four-bladed propeller. The first examples entered service in April 1943, and the Mk III remained in production until mid-1945.

Right: Supermarine Seafire Mk IB

Vought F4U/FG-1 Corsair USA

Type: single-engined monoplane fighter　　**Accommodation:** pilot

Development/History

Designed as a lightweight fighter tailored around the most powerful piston engine then available, Vought's prototype XF4U-1 was ordered by the US Navy in June 1938 following a study of their V-166 proposal. In order to harness the immense power of the Pratt & Whitney XR-2800 Double Wasp engine, the largest diameter propeller ever fitted to a fighter up to that point in aeronautical history had to be bolted on the front of the prototype – sufficient ground clearance for the prop was achieved through the use of a distinctive inverted gull wing. The future looked rosy for the aircraft, but modifications incorporated into the design as a result of lessons learned in combat over Europe detrimentally affected the Corsair. As a result of these problems, it was left to land-based Marine Corps units to debut the aircraft in combat in early 1943 – the Royal Navy's Fleet Air Arm also commenced operations with the Corsair that same year, but crucially from the decks of carriers. By mid-1944 Vought had rectified the handling problems, and the Corsair became suitable for deck operations with the US Navy. Unlike other navy fighters, the Corsair enjoyed a prosperous

postwar career, with both Vought- and Goodyear-built aircraft remaining in service until after the Korean War. Indeed, the final F4U-7 (built for the French *Aéronavale*) did not roll off the Vought production line until 31 January 1952, this aircraft being the 12,571st, and last, Corsair built.

Specification (all dimensions and performance data for F4U-1D)

Dimensions:

Length: 32 ft 9.5 in (9.99 m)
Wingspan: 40 ft 11.75 in (12.49 m)
Height: 15 ft 0.25 in (4.58 m)

Weights:

Empty: 8873 lb (4025 kg)
Max T/O: 13 846 lb (6280 kg)

Performance:

Max Speed: 392 mph (631 kmh)
Range: 1562 miles (2514 km)
Powerplant: Pratt & Whitney R-2800-8 Double Wasp
Output: 2000 hp (1491 kW)

First Flight Date:

29 May 1940

Armament:

six 0.50 in machine guns in wings; two 1000 lb (454 kg) bombs or eight rocket projectiles externally

Operators:

New Zealand, UK, USA

Production:

12 571 (all models)

Right: Vought Corsair II JT228 of the Fleet Air Arm

Westland Whirlwind I UK

Type: twin-engined monoplane fighter　　**Accommodation:** pilot

Development/History

Built to a 1935 Air Ministry specification calling for a twin-engined fighter, the Whirlwind became the first of its type to enter service with the RAF in mid-1940. At the heart of the Westland design was its impressive quartet of 20 mm cannon, which were fitted in response to the specification's stipulation that the chosen aircraft had to be a 'cannon fighter'. Well thought out and beautifully crafted, the Whirlwind also possessed excellent handling characteristics and an impressive top speed at all operational altitudes. The aircraft looked to have a promising future, but sadly it was quickly put behind schedule by the unreliability of its unique Peregrine engines. Developed from the highly successful Kestrel inline engine of the 1930s, the Peregrine was never able to repeat the success of its forebear, or the superlative Merlin, which utilised a similar V12 inline layout. Indeed, many at Westland pleaded to be able to swap the Peregrines for Merlins, but the latter were in short supply in 1940, and all that were produced were channelled towards the Spitfire and Hurricane. The Whirlwind was left to struggle on, and the first production examples finally reached the frontline in mid-

1940 – eight months behind schedule. By 1941 it was obvious that single-seat fighters could perform all the tasks demanded of Fighter Command, so Whirlwind production was stopped after just 112 aircraft had been delivered to the air force. Surviving Whirlwinds were converted into fighter-bombers in June 1941, and they operated in this role over the Channel until 1943.

Specification

Dimensions:

Length: 32 ft 3 in (9.83 m)
Wingspan: 45 ft 0 in (13.72 m)
Height: 10 ft 6 in (3.20 m)

Weights:

Empty: 8310 lb (3770 kg)
Max T/O: 11 388 lb (5165 kg)

Performance:

Max Speed: 360 mph (579 kmh)
Range: 800 miles (1287 km)
Powerplants: two Rolls-Royce Peregrine I engines
Output: 1770 hp (1320 kW)

First Flight Date:

11 October 1938

Armament:

four 20 mm cannon in nose; 1000 lb (454 kg) bombload under wings

Operators:

UK

Production:

114

Right: Westland Whirlwind Mk I P6997

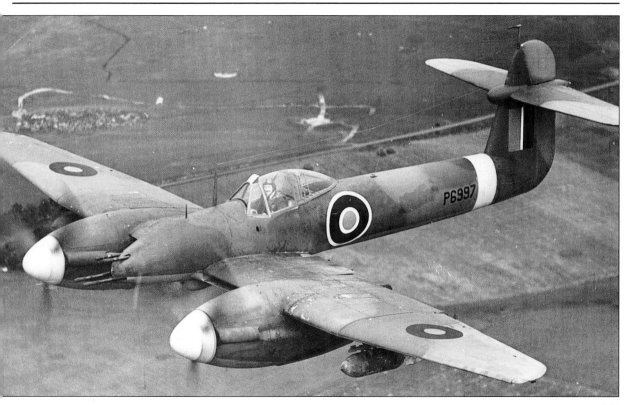

Yakovlev Yak-1/-7 USSR

Type: single-engined monoplane fighter   **Accommodation:** pilot

Development/History

Yakovlev were responsible for producing the most successful series of fighter aircraft used by the Soviet Union during World War 2, and the first to enter service was the Yak-1. Built in response to a 1938 requirement for a single-engined 'frontal' fighter, Yakovlev's I-26 was chosen as the winner from several proposals put forward. Later redesignated Yak-1 in recognition of its design bureau, the small fighter was of mixed wood and metal construction and powered by the ubiquitous Klimov M-105F engine. The first aircraft to enter service were considered underpowered and overweight, and Yakovlev set about lightening the fighter (by cutting down the rear fuselage decking), and fitting the more powerful M-105PF engine in place of the F-model. However, it would be early 1943 before the first revised Yak-1Ms reached the frontline, and in the meantime the standard Yak-1 carried the fight to the Germans. Some 400 were available when the USSR was invaded, and production was briefly halted when the entire Yakovlev production line was shifted 1000 miles further east to avoid being captured. The very similar Yak-7 was initially built as a two-seat trainer variant, but its simpler construction,

Specification (all dimensions and performance data for Yak-7B)

Dimensions:
Length: 27 ft 9.5 in (8.47 m)
Wingspan: 32 ft 9.75 in (10.00 m)
Height: 9 ft 0.25 in (2.75 m)

Weights:
Empty: 5467 lb (2480 kg)
Loaded Weight: 6680 lb (3030 kg)

Performance:
Max Speed: 382 mph (615 kmh)
Range: 510 miles (820 km)
Powerplant: Klimov M-105PF
Output: 1260 hp (940 kW)

Armament:
one 20 mm cannon in propeller hub and two 12.7 mm machine guns in upper cowling; provision for 441 lb (200 kg) bomb load or six 82 mm rockets under wings

First Flight Date:
13 January 1940 (I-26/Yak-1) and 4 July 1940 (UTI-26/Yak-7V)

Operators:
France, Poland, USSR

Production:
8721 Yak-1s and 6399 Yak-7s

lighter weight and resulting performance also saw it chosen for the low-level fighter-bomber role (in single-seat configuration, with the space previously occupied by a seat being filled by an additional fuel tank). Later Yak-7Bs also incorporated the numerous upgrades featured in the Yak-1M. Production of both models had ceased by late 1943.

Right: GAZ 292-built Yakovlev Yak-7B in mid-1942

Yakovlev Yak-9 USSR

Type: single-engined fighter   **Accommodation:** pilot

Development/History

The original Yak-9 appeared in frontline service in late 1942, the aircraft being a lightweight version of the Yak-7, which had been the VVS's staple fighter since the end of 1941. By mid-1944, the Yak-9 outnumbered all other fighters in service on the Eastern Front, with a handful of variants fulfilling the long-range interception role, fighter-bomber tasks, nightfighting and close-support missions. The second generation Yak-9U/P version of the venerable fighter started development in late 1942, when a standard airframe had its Klimov M-105 engine replaced by the appreciably more powerful M-107 powerplant sourced from the same manufacturer. Aerodynamic improvements were also made to the overall fuselage, and plywood skinning replaced with light alloy. Designated the Yak-9U, the new fighter eventually reached VVS units in the final months of the war, its service entry having been drastically delayed due to engine problems. Indeed the first aircraft delivered by Yakovlev had to rely on the M-105 for motive power. Further development of the Yak-9 continued immediately postwar, with an enhanced version – cannon-armed Yak-9P –

seeing use not only with the VVS, but also a number of other communist-bloc air forces, including North Korea. Production finally ceased in 1947 after 3900 Yak-9U/Ps (out of an overall total of 16,769 Yak-9s built) had been delivered.

Specification (all dimensions and performance data for Yak-9D)

Dimensions:
Length: 28 ft 0.25 in (8.55 m)
Wingspan: 31 ft 11.5 in (9.74 m)
Height: 9 ft 10 in (3.00 m)

Weights:
Empty: 5100 lb (2313 kg)
Loaded Weight: 6988 lb (3170 kg)

Performance:
Max Speed: 374 mph (602 kmh)
Range: 870 miles (1400 km)
Powerplant: Klimov M-105PF-3
Output: 1360 hp (1014 kW)

Armament:
one 20 mm cannon in propeller hub and two 12.7 mm machine guns in upper cowling; provision for 441 lb (200 kg) bomb load under wings

First Flight Date:
Late December 1942

Operators:
France, Poland, USSR

Production:
16 769

Right: Yakovlev Yak-9D in the summer of 1943

188

Yakovlev Yak-3 USSR

Type: single-engined fighter   **Accommodation:** pilot

Development/History

The second Yakovlev aircraft to be designated the Yak-3 (the first was abandoned in the autumn of 1941 due to poor engine reliability and a shortage of suitable building materials), this machine was built to fulfil a VVS requirement for an agile fighter capable of achieving its maximum performance at low altitude. By meeting these criteria, the fighter bestowed upon the Soviet Air Force the ability to maintain air superiority immediately over the battlefield – something that the Luftwaffe had enjoyed for much of the war on the Eastern Front. Utilising a modified Yak-1M fitted with a smaller wing, the prototypes completed their service trials in October 1943, by which time a small pre-series run of aircraft had been put into production at GAZ 286 at Kamensk Ural'ski. The Yak-3 was not officially cleared for full-scale production until June 1944, and the small number of regiments which rapidly re-equipped with the fighter soon proved the fighter's superiority over its Luftwaffe counterparts in a number of aerial engagements – it was so dominant in combat that the Luftwaffe ordered that its fighter pilots avoid intercepting any Yaks encountered

Specification

Dimensions:
Length: 27 ft 10.25 in (8.49 m)
Wingspan: 30 ft 2.25 in (9.20 m)
Height: 7 ft 11.25 in (2.42 m)

Weights:
Empty: 4641 lb (2105 kg)
Max T/O: 5864 lb (2660 kg)

Performance:
Max Speed: 407 mph (655 kmh)
Range: 559 miles (900 km)
Powerplant: Klimov M-105PF
Output: 1650 hp (1230 kW)

Armament:
one 20 mm cannon in propeller hub and two 12.7 mm machine guns in upper cowling

First Flight Date:
late 1942

Operators:
France, Poland, USSR

Production:
4848

below 16,400 ft (5000 m). The Yak-3 remained in production until early 1946, by which time 4848 had been built.

Right: A Yakovlev Yak-3 of the famous Normandie-Niémen squadron